# Growth and Income Distribution
## *Essays in Economic Theory*

### LUIGI L. PASINETTI

## CAMBRIDGE UNIVERSITY PRESS

### CAMBRIDGE

LONDON · NEW YORK · MELBOURNE

Published by the Syndics of the Cambridge University Press
The Pitt Building, Trumpington Street, Cambridge CB2 1RP
Bentley House, 200 Euston Road, London NW1 2DB
32 East 57th Street, New York, NY 10022, USA
296 Beaconsfield Parade, Middle Park, Melbourne 3206, Australia

© Cambridge University Press 1974

Library of Congress catalogue card number 74-76579

ISBN 0 521 20474 7 hard covers
ISBN 0 521 29543 2 paperback

First published 1974
Reprinted 1975, 1978
First paperback edition 1979

Printed and bound in Great Britain by
Redwood Burn Limited
Trowbridge & Esher

# Contents

# Contents

# Preface

The essays collected in this book (with the exception of Essay VI) were conceived in the years 1958–62, in a period when I moved, in quick succession, from the University of Cambridge, England, to Harvard University in the U.S.A., to Nuffield College, Oxford, and then back to Cambridge again. Essays I, III, and V have been published already, and are here reprinted by kind permission of the *Review of Economic Studies*, the *Oxford Economic Papers* and *l'industria*. I am reproducing them without alterations, except for obvious errors and misprints and a few very minor excisions – mainly footnotes, to avoid repetition. Essays II, IV and VI appear here for the first time. Essays II and IV contain material which I have used in some of my lectures at the University of Cambridge, as many of my pupils will no doubt recognize. Essay VI on the other hand is much more recent, and is in a sense quite distinct from all the others; it was mainly written during my stay as Wesley Clair Mitchell Research Professor of Economics at Columbia University, New York, in 1971–72.

All the essays have in common the same basic conception of the working of the economic system and are therefore complementary to one another. I have sandwiched Essays II and IV in between the previously published essays to provide the missing links – an exploration of the deep Classical, and particularly Ricardian, foundations of Keynesian and post-Keynesian economic theory. As is shown in Essay II, Keynes' theory of effective demand, which has remained so impervious to reconciliation with marginal economic theory, raises almost no problem when directly inserted into the earlier discussions of the Classical economists. Similarly, as is shown in Essay IV, the post-Keynesian theories of economic growth and income distribution, which have required so many artificial assumptions in the efforts to reconcile them with marginal productivity theory, encounter almost no difficulty when directly grafted on to Classical economic dynamics. I have appended

Essay VI to answer a series of questions which have arisen from a theorem contained in Essay V. After all the discussions, a final conclusion emerges on the basic forces determining the rate of profit in the process of economic growth.

I have tried, in the whole book, to insist on the positive and constructive aspects of Classical and post-Keynesian theories. Polemics has been left aside and criticism kept to a minimum. I hope I have succeeded in giving unity and homogeneity to the whole, and in providing a coherent picture of so much of the Keynesian and post-Keynesian economic thinking that has recently originated in Cambridge.

I am glad to take this opportunity to express my deep gratitude to that remarkable group of thinkers – Richard Kahn, Nicholas Kaldor, Joan Robinson and Piero Sraffa – whom I had the rare fortune of meeting, discussing with so often, and then being associated with, in Cambridge, which has been to me the most stimulating place I could possibly imagine for progressive thought in economic theory. To the reader of the present essays it will appear only inadequately how much I owe to them. The warning, therefore, becomes more than usually necessary that the conception of Keynesian economic theory that emerges from the following pages must not be taken as necessarily expressing their views. Though inspired by them, I alone must take full responsibility.

My thanks also go to all teachers, colleagues and pupils with whom I had countless discussions. It would take too long to list them all. But I should like to thank particularly: Richard Goodwin, James Duesenberry, Franco Modigliani, James Meade and Robin Marris.

I am grateful for financial support to the institutions where I have been working, but especially to: King's College, Cambridge; Nuffield College, Oxford; and the Department of Economics of Columbia University, New York.

L.L.P.

*King's College, Cambridge*
*December 1973*

# I

# A mathematical formulation of the Ricardian system[*]

Since his own time, David Ricardo has always occupied a privileged place among economists, even in periods when economic analysis has been developing along paths very different from the ones he pursued. It has never been easy, however, for Ricardo's many interpreters, to state his complete system in a rigorous and concise form, and the reason lies in the peculiarity of some of the concepts he used, which are not always defined in an unambiguous way. These concepts have encountered strong criticisms almost at any time, while – on the other hand – the bold analyses they made possible were exerting a sort of fascinating attraction.

In this essay, criticism is left aside and the more constructive approach is taken of stating explicitly the assumptions needed in order to eliminate the ambiguities. Then, the Ricardian system is shown to be very neat and even suitable for a mathematical formulation, with all the advantages of conciseness, rigour and clarity. The task is undertaken in sections 4 to 9, which form the main part of the paper (part II). To avoid digressions and lengthy references there, the difficulties Ricardo was faced with and the basic features of his theories are briefly reviewed in the first three introductory sections (part I).

I

## 1. *Theory of value*

The theory of value represents the most toilsome part of Ricardo's theoretical system and in our mathematical formulation it will entail the crudest assumptions. At the time it was put forward, the theory soon became the main target of the criticisms, which Ricardo tried to

[*] Originally published in *The Review of Economic Studies*, vol. XXVII, no. 2, February 1960, pp. 78–98.

1

answer by re-writing twice (in the second and in the third edition) the chapter 'on value' of his *Principles*.[1] No fundamental change was introduced, however, and the three versions represent different ways of framing (in the light of the criticisms) a theory of value which remains essentially the same.[2]

The theory is fundamentally based on the cost of production measured in terms of quantity of labour. Utility[3] is considered to be absolutely essential to, but not a measure of, exchangeable value. To commodities which derive their value from 'scarcity alone'[4] (e.g., rare paintings) only a few words are devoted – they are not considered relevant for economic analysis; Ricardo is concerned only with commodities which are the outcome of a process of production. And of these commodities he is concerned with finding the 'primary and natural price', as against 'the accidental and temporary deviations of the actual or market price'.[5] He begins by restating Adam Smith's proposition that 'in the early stages of society, the exchangeable value of commodities . . . depends . . . on the comparative quantity of labour expended on each'.[6] Then, he takes a new and striking step by asserting that *the mentioned proposition is valid in general* and not only in the early stages of society, as Smith claimed. His argument may be roughly expressed in the following way. Suppose two commodities, *A* and *B*, the first of which requires the work of one worker for one year to be produced and the second the work of two workers for one year (the capital employed being just the amount of wages to be anticipated to the workers). Whatever the rate of profit may be, either 10 per cent or

[1] David Ricardo, *On the Principles of Political Economy and Taxation* (cit. as *Principles*). All references to Ricardo's works in this essay refer to the edition prepared by Piero Sraffa, *The Works and Correspondence of David Ricardo*, 11 vols, Cambridge, 1951–73, (cit. as *Works*).

[2] This is a view to which recently Mr Sraffa has given full support (*Works*, vol. I, Introduction, pp. xxxvii and ff.). Fragments of an early version of the Ricardian theory of value can be traced in Ricardo's early writings and in some letters (see the evidence given by Mr Sraffa, *Works*, vol. I, p. xxxi). It seems that Ricardo tried at the beginning to measure the relevant variables of his system in terms of a main agricultural commodity, namely corn, claiming that this commodity has the property of being both the capital and the product and, therefore, makes it possible to determine the ratio of profit to capital in physical terms, without any question of evaluation. This position was, however, very vulnerable and will not be considered in this essay, as Ricardo abandoned it before writing the *Principles*.

[3] Needless to say, the term 'utility' has for Ricardo, and in general for the Classics, a different meaning than for us to-day. It simply refers to the 'value in use' of a commodity as opposed to its 'value in exchange'. See *Principles*, p. 11.

[4] *Principles*, p. 12.  [5] *Principles*, p. 88.

[6] *Principles*, p. 12.

20 per cent or 30 per cent, the profit on the second commodity always is twice as much as on the first commodity; hence the relative price of the two goods always comes out as equal to the ratio of the quantities of labour required to obtain each of them.[7] If a 'commodity could be found, which now and at all times required precisely the same quantity of labour to produce it, that commodity would be of an unvarying value'[8]: it would be an *invariable standard* in terms of which the value of all commodities could be expressed.

This formulation of the theory, of course, did not remain unchallenged. Strong objections were immediately raised (by Malthus, McCulloch, Torrens and others) which may be summarized as follows. Let us suppose, returning to the mentioned example, that the production of commodity *B* requires the work of one worker for two years instead of the work of two workers for one year. In this case, Ricardo's principle no longer applies because, owing to the profits becoming themselves capital at the end of the first year, a change in the rate of profit *does* imply a change in the relative price of the two commodities, even though the relative quantities of labour required by them remain the same.[9] Ricardo could not ignore these objections and already in the first edition of the *Principles* he allowed for some exceptions to his general rule. All exceptions – as he later explained in a letter – 'come under one of time',[10] but he preferred discussing them, in the third edition of the *Principles*, under three groups (i. different proportions of fixed and circulating capital, ii. unequal durability of fixed capital, iii. unequal rapidity with which the circulating capital ·returns to its employer). However, while allowing for exceptions, Ricardo kept the fundamentals of his theory and tried to overcome the objections by appealing to the order of magnitude of the deviations caused by the exceptions, which he considered as responsible only for minor departures from his general rule. In the previous example, for instance, the modification introduced by the possibility that the same quantity of labour on *B* might be employed in one year or in two different years amounts simply to the effects caused by the capitalization of the profits calculated on the wages of the first year. Ricardo holds that this is a

[7] *Principles*, pp. 24 and ff.

[8] *Principles*, version of editions 1 and 2, see p. 17, footnote 3.

[9] An *invariable standard of value* presents therefore two distinct difficulties. First of all there is the difficulty of finding a commodity which 'now and at all times requires precisely the same quantity of labour to produce it'. Secondly, even if such a commodity were to be found, there is the further difficulty that its value would change with changes in the distribution of income.

[10] Letter to McCulloch, *Works*, vol. VIII, p. 193.

difference of minor importance.[11] Therefore, the conclusion is, the theory of value as stated in terms of quantities of labour, and independently of the distribution of income among the classes of the society, does hold, if not exactly, at least as a very good approximation ('the nearest approximation to truth'[12]). With this premise, Ricardo considers as 'the principal problem of Political Economy' that of determining 'the laws which regulate the distribution'.[13]

## 2. *Theory of distribution*

The participants in the process of production are grouped by Ricardo into three classes: landlords who provide land, capitalists[14] who provide capital and workers who provide labour. Total production is entirely determined by technical conditions but its division among the three classes – under the form of rent, profit and wages – is determined by the inter-action of many technical, economic and demographic factors. All Ricardo's analysis on this subject refers to what he calls the *natural* prices of rent, profits and wages. Divergencies of market prices from their natural level are considered only as temporary and unimportant deviations.

Rent, namely 'that portion of the produce of the earth which is paid to the landlords for the use of the original and indestructible power of the soil'[15] is determined by technical factors. The technical property that different pieces of land have different fertility and that successive applications of labour to the same quantity of land yield smaller and smaller amounts of product (law of diminishing returns) makes of rent

[11] *Principles*, pp. 36 and ff.

[12] Letter to Malthus, *Works*, vol. VIII, p. 279; see also Sraffa's Introduction, *Works*, vol. I, p. xl. With the acceptance of criticisms, between the first and the third edition of the *Principles*, also the choice of a 'standard of value' became more difficult. Ricardo reacted to the complication by changing his definitions. In the first edition of the *Principles* he regarded as 'standard' a commodity which would require at any time the same amount of unassisted labour (unassisted by capital); in the third edition he mentions a 'commodity produced with such proportions of the two kinds of capital [fixed and circulating] as approach nearest to the average quantity employed in the production of most commodities' (*Principles*, p. 63 and p. 45; see also *Works*, Introduction by Mr Sraffa, vol. I, p. xlii and ff.). Ricardo considered one year a good average and thought that perhaps gold could be the commodity that most closely approaches the requirement of an *invariable standard*. (*Principles*, p. 45.)

[13] *Principles*, p. 3.

[14] Ricardo calls them alternatively 'farmers' or 'manufacturers', according as he refers to agricultural or to industrial capitalists.

[15] *Principles*, p. 67.

a *net gain* for the landlords. Therefore, rent does not enter Ricardo's theory of value – it is a deduction from the total product. The value of commodities is determined by the quantity of labour employed on the marginal portion of land – that portion of land which yields no rent.

Wages are not related to the contribution of labour to the process of production, as in the modern theories they normally are. Like all economists of his time, Ricardo relates the level of wages to the physiological necessity of workers and their families to live and reproduce themselves. He is convinced that in any particular state of society there exists a *real* wage-rate (so to speak, a certain *basket of goods*) which can be considered as the 'natural price of labour'. It need not necessarily be at a strict *subsistence level*[16] (the minimum physiological necessities of life); but at that level which in a given country and in a given state of society, besides allowing workers to live, induces them to perpetuate themselves 'without either increase or diminution'.[17] When capitalists accumulate capital, demand for labour increases and the market wage-rate rises above its natural level. However, Ricardo believes that such a situation cannot be other than a temporary one because, as the conditions of workers become 'flourishing and happy', they 'rear a healthy and numerous family'[18] and the growth of population again brings back the real wage-rate to its *natural* level. It is very impressive to notice how strongly Ricardo is convinced of the operation of this mechanism. To be precise, he always speaks of a process which will operate 'ultimately' but the emphasis on it is so strong that his analysis is always carried on *as if* the response were almost immediate.

Profits, finally, represent a residual. Rent being determined by the produce of the marginal land put into cultivation, and the wage-rate by non-economic factors, what remains of the total production is retained, under the form of profit, by the capitalists, who are the organizers of the process of production. The capitalists are assumed to be always intent on moving their capital towards any sector of the economy that shows a tendency to yield a rate of profit above the average. This behaviour ensures the equalization of the rate of profit (after risk) all over the economy.

---

[16] 'The natural price of labour – Ricardo says – varies at different times, in the same country, and very materially differs in different countries. It essentially depends on the habits and customs of the people . . . Many of the conveniences – Ricardo adds – now enjoyed in an English cottage would have been thought luxuries in an earlier period of our history.' (*Principles*, pp. 96–7.)

[17] *Principles*, p. 93.

[18] *Principles*, p. 94.

### 3. *Theory of economic growth*

Economic growth is brought about essentially by the capitalists. The three classes in which Ricardo divides society have different peculiar characteristics. Landlords are considered as an 'unproductive class'[19] of wealthy people who become richer and richer, and consume almost all their incomes in *luxury-goods*. Workers also consume everything they get but in a different kind of goods – 'necessaries' – in order to live. Capitalists, on the other hand, are the *entrepreneurs* of the system. They represent the 'productive class'[20] of society. Very thrifty, they consume a small amount of what they obtain and devote their profits to capital accumulation.

The process of transforming profits into capital, however, cannot go on indefinitely. Owing to the diminishing returns of new capital (and labour) applied to the same quantity of land, or to less fertile lands, rent increases over time, in real and in money terms, the *money* wage-rate increases too[21], and consequently the profit-rate continuously falls.[22] When the rate of profit has fallen to zero, capitalists are prevented from accumulating any more; the growth process stops and the system reaches a *stationary state*. As a matter of fact – Ricardo adds – the stationary state will be reached *before* the extreme point where all profits have disappeared because, at a certain minimum rate of profit, the capitalists will lose any inducement to accumulate. The final outcome (the stationary state) is postponed in time by new inventions and discoveries, which increase the productivity of labour, but it is Ricardo's opinion that it will eventually be attained.

### II

### 4. *'Natural' equilibrium in a two-commodity system*

It has been mentioned that Ricardo distinguishes two groups of commodities produced in the economy: 'necessaries' – or, we may call them wage-goods – and 'luxuries'. The most simple Ricardian system we can conceive of is, therefore, one where each of the two groups is reduced to one commodity. Let us begin with this case and make the following assumptions:

---

[19/20] *Principles*, p. 270.

[21] How this happens will appear very clearly in the mathematical treatment of the following sections.

[22] *Principles*, especially chapters VI and XXI.

(i) the system produces only one type of wage-good, let us call it corn;

(ii) to produce corn, it takes exactly one year;

(iii) capital consists entirely of the wage-bill; in other words, it is only circulating capital, which takes one year to be re-integrated;

(iv) there does exist an invariable standard of value, namely a commodity, let us call it gold – a luxury-good – , which at any time and place always requires the same quantity of labour to be produced. Its process of production also takes one year. Prices are expressed in terms of such a commodity and the monetary unit is that quantity of gold which is produced by the labour of one worker in one year.

The Ricardian system can now be stated in terms of equations. Taking the quantity of land in existence as given and supposing that its technical characteristics (fertility and possibilities of intensive exploitation) are known, the production of corn can be expressed by a technical production function, which we may assume to be continuously differentiable:

$$X_1 = f(N_1), \tag{1.1}$$

where: $X_1$ = physical quantity of corn produced in one year; $N_1$ = number of workers employed in the corn production;

with the following properties:

$$f(0) \geqslant 0, \tag{1.1a}$$

$$f'(0) > \bar{x}, \tag{1.1b}$$

where: $\bar{x}$ = natural wage-rate in terms of corn,

$$f''(N_1) < 0. \tag{1.1c}$$

The first inequality means that when no labour is employed, land is supposed to produce either something or nothing at all (negative production is excluded). The meaning of (1.1b) is that, at least when the economic system begins to operate and workers are employed on the most fertile piece of land, they must produce more than what is strictly necessary for their support, otherwise the whole economic system would never come into existence. Finally, (1.1c) expresses the law of diminishing returns.

The production function for gold is much simpler:

$$X_2 = \alpha N_2, \tag{1.2}$$

7

where: $X_2$ = physical quantity of gold produced in one year; $N_2$ = number of workers employed in the production of gold; $\alpha$ = physical quantity of gold produced by one worker in one year ($\alpha > 0$).

The following equations are self-explanatory:[23]

$$N = N_1 + N_2, \tag{1.3}$$

$$W = N\,x, \tag{1.4}$$

$$K = W, \tag{1.5}$$

$$R = f(N_1) - N_1 f'(N_1), \tag{1.6}$$

$$P_1 = X_1 - R - N_1 x, \tag{1.7}$$

where: $N$ = total number of workers; $N_1$ = agricultural workers; $N_2$ = workers in the gold industry; $W$ = total wage-bill, in terms of physical units of corn; $x$ = real wage-rate (corn); $K$ = physical stock of capital (corn); $R$ = yearly rent, in real terms (corn); $P_1$ = yearly total profits, in real terms (corn), in the corn producing sector.

All variables introduced so far are in physical terms. Turning now to the determination of values, we have:

$$p_1 X_1 - p_1 R = N_1, \tag{1.8}$$

$$p_2 X_2 = N_2, \tag{1.9}$$

where: $p_1$ = price of corn; $p_2$ = price of gold.

Equations (1.8) and (1.9) are very important in the Ricardian system. They state that the value of the yearly product, *after deduction of rent*, is determined by the quantity of labour required to produce it. In our case, owing to the definition of the monetary unit, the value of the product, after paying rent, is exactly equal to the number of workers

---

[23] Equation (1.6) may not appear so evident as the other equations. Let me state, therefore, an alternative way of writing it. As explained in section 2, rent represents for Ricardo a net gain for the owners of the more fertile lands with respect to the owners of the marginal land (the land which yields no rent). Therefore, when $N_1$ workers are employed on land, the resulting total rent can be expressed as a sum of all the *net gains* for the non-marginal land-owners. In analytical terms:

$$R = f(0) + \int_0^{N_1} [f'(y) - f'(N_1)]\,\mathrm{d}y, \tag{1.6a}$$

where $f(0)$, from (1.1a), is the produce that the land-owners can get from land without renting it, i.e. without any labour being employed. By solving the integral appearing in (1.6a), we obtain:

$$R = f(0) + f(N_1) - f(0) - N_1 f'(N_1),$$

which is exactly equation (1.6).

employed. From (1.1), (1.2) and (1.6), equations (1.8) and (1.9) may be also written:

$$p_1 = \frac{N_1}{X_1 - R} = \frac{1}{f'(N_1)},$$  (1.8a)

$$p_2 = \frac{1}{\alpha}.$$  (1.9a)

Profits in the gold industry and total profits in the economy emerge as:

$$p_2 P_2 = p_2 X_2 - N_2 p_1 x,$$  (1.10)

$$\pi = p_1 X_1 + p_2 X_2 - p_1 R - p_1 W,$$  (1.11)

where: $P_2 =$ profits, in terms of physical units of gold, in the gold industry; $\pi =$ total profits, in terms of the standard of value.

After substituting from (1.1)–(1.10), equation (1.11) may be also written:

$$\pi = (N_1 + N_2)(1 - x\,p_1).$$  (1.11a)

At this point, the equations contain a theory of value and a theory of distribution but not yet a theory of expenditure. Since Ricardo assumes that all incomes are spent (Say's law), to determine the composition of total expenditure only one equation is necessary in the present model, specifying the production of one of the two commodities. Then the quantity produced of the other commodity turns out to be implicitly determined, as *total* production has already been functionally specified. The Ricardian theory is very primitive on this point. Workers are supposed to spend their income on necessities (corn, in our case) capitalists on capital accumulation (corn again, in our case) and land-owners on luxuries. Hence the determining equation is:[24]

$$p_2 X_2 = p_1 R.$$  (1.12)

Let us also write:

---

[24] To be precise, we should allow for a minimum of necessities to be bought by the land-owners. This *minimum*, however, introduces only a constant into the analysis without modifying its essential features. For simplicity, therefore, the procedure is followed of neglecting the constant, which amounts to considering the minimum as negligible and supposing that the whole rent is spent on luxuries. Similarly, a minimum of luxuries might be allowed to be bought by the capitalists. This *minimum* also will be considered as negligible.

$$w = p_1 x, \tag{1.13}$$

$$r = \frac{\pi}{p_1 K}, \tag{1.14}$$

where: $w$ = monetary wage-rate; $r$ = rate of profit.

So far 16 variables have appeared: $X_1$, $X_2$, $N_1$, $N_2$, $N$, $W$, $x$, $K$, $R$, $P_1$, $P_2$, $\pi$, $p_1$, $p_2$, $w$, $r$, but only 14 equations. Two more equations are needed in order to determine the system. In a situation which Ricardo considers as *natural*, the following two data have to be added:

$$x = \bar{x} > 0, \tag{1.15}$$

$$K = \bar{K} > 0, \tag{1.16}$$

where: $\bar{x}$ = *natural* real wage-rate, defined as that wage-rate which keeps population constant; $\bar{K}$ = given stock of capital at the beginning of the year.

The system is now complete and determinate.[25] It can be easily demonstrated (see the appendix) that properties (1.1*a*), (1.1*b*), (1.1*c*) and the inequalities put on (1.15)–(1.16) are sufficient conditions to ensure the existence and uniqueness of non-negative solutions. We may consider, therefore, the system of equations (1.1)–(1.16) as expressing the *natural* equilibrium of the Ricardian system.[26]

### 5. *Some characteristics of the Ricardian system*

Already at this stage, the system of the previous section clearly shows some of the most typical characteristics of the Ricardian model. First of all, it contains a theory of value which is completely and (owing to our explicit assumptions) rigorously independent of distribution. From equations (1.8*a*) and (1.9*a*), it appears that the value of commodities

[25] It may be interesting to notice that equations (1.1), (1.4), (1.5), (1.6), (1.7), (1.15) and (1.16), taken by themselves, form an extremely simplified but determined Ricardian system expressed in terms of corn, where any question of evaluation has not yet arisen, corn being the single commodity produced. This is the system which has been used by Mr Kaldor in his article 'Alternative Theories of Distribution', *The Review of Economic Studies*, 1955–6, pp. 83–100.

[26] To justify the terminology, let me mention that in his article 'On the Notion of Equilibrium and Disequilibrium', *The Review of Economic Studies*, 1935–6, pp. 100–5, Professor Ragnar Frisch distinguishes two types of equilibria: *stationary* and *moving*. The *natural* equilibrium of the Ricardian system is not a stationary one, as will be seen in a moment; it belongs to the *moving* type. Professor Frisch, in that article, describes a somewhat similar situation for the Wicksellian *natural* rate of interest.

depends exclusively on technical factors (more precisely, on the quantity of labour required to produce them) and on nothing else – a pure labour theory of value.

Moreover, the equations show that wage-goods and luxury-goods play two different roles in the system. The production function for the wage-commodity turns out to be of fundamental importance, while the conditions of production of the luxury-good, expressed by $\alpha$, have in the system a very limited influence. As can be easily found out (see also the appendix), the solutions for *all* variables, except $p_2$, depend on the function $f(N_1)$ or on its first derivative, while the constant $\alpha$ only enters the solutions for $X_2$ and $p_2$. As a consequence, the rate of profit and the money wage-rate are determined by the conditions of production of wage-goods and are entirely independent of the conditions of production of luxury-goods.[27] It follows, for example – to mention one problem of concern to Ricardo – that a tax on wage-goods would affect all the participants in the process of production by changing both the money wage-rate and the rate of profit (as can be inferred from equations (1.13a) and (1.14a)), while a tax on luxury-goods would affect only the purchasers of these goods, because it leaves the rates of profit and of wages entirely unaffected.[28]

### 6. The market solutions and the attainment of the 'natural' equilibrium

Ricardo admits that the market outcomes may not necessarily coincide with those of his 'natural' equilibrium, but he considers two types of mechanisms which make the former converge towards the latter. First,

[27] This can be seen more clearly by re-writing (1.13) and (1.14) after substitution from (1.4), (1.8a), (1.11a), (1.15). We obtain:

$$w = \frac{\bar{x}}{f'(N_1)}, \qquad (1.13a); \qquad r = \frac{f'(N_1)}{\bar{x}} - 1. \qquad (1.14a)$$

[28] The independence of the rate of profit from the conditions of production of luxury-goods is a property of all the theoretical models which use the distinction between wage- and luxury-goods. In plain words, it is due to the peculiarity that wage-goods are necessary to produce any type of goods, while luxury-goods are not. Mr Sraffa pointed out to me that the property was first discovered by Ladislaus von Bortkiewicz ('Zur Berichtigung der Grundlegenden theoretischen Konstruktion von Marx im dritten Band des 'Kapital'', in *Jahrbücher für Nationalökonomie und Statistik*, July 1907. An English translation can be found as an appendix to the volume *Karl Marx and the Close of His System*, by E. Böhm-Bawerk and *Böhm-Bawerk's Criticism of Marx*, by R. Hilferding, translated and edited by P. M. Sweezy, New York, 1949). From the present mathematical formulation, the property comes out very simply and clearly. [In Mr Sraffa's more recent terminology (*Production of Commodities by means of Commodities*, Cambridge, 1960), the wage-goods are *basic* commodities and the luxury-goods are *non-basic* commodities.]

he mentions the behaviour of the capitalists, whose readiness to move their capital towards the most profitable sectors of the economy always causes the rates of profit to equalize in all sectors. Secondly, he considers the increase of the working population in response to increases in wages. About the first of these two processes, Ricardo does not really say much more than what is said here. He does not find it useful to enter into complicated details (and in this case they would have been very complicated indeed for him, who did not possess a demand theory). Simply he allows for the process and carries on his analysis (the system (1.1)–(1.16)) on the assumption that the equalization of the rates of profit has already been permanently achieved. On the other hand, his analysis is more explicit, and can be clearly formulated, on the second type of mechanism.

At the beginning of our hypothetical year, what is really given (besides capital) is not the wage-rate but the number of workers. Therefore, the solutions determined by the market (supposing the rates of profit already equalized) are given by the system (1.1)–(1.14), (1.16) plus the following equality (replacing (1.15)):

$$N = \bar{N}, \tag{1.15a}$$

where: $\bar{N} =$ number of workers at the beginning of the year.

The system is again complete and determinate but the wage-rate has now become a variable and has a solution (the market solution). Ricardo is firmly convinced that this solution can only be a temporary and unstable one because, if it comes out different from the *natural* wage-rate ($\bar{x}$), the population will adjust itself in such a way as to bring the two rates together. Analytically, the mechanism may be expressed as follows:

$$\frac{\mathrm{d}N}{\mathrm{d}t} = F(x - \bar{x}), \tag{1.17}$$

where: $t$ denotes time and $x$ the wage-rate resulting from the system (1.1)–(1.14), (1.15a), (1.16);
with the properties[29]:

$$F(0) = 0,$$
$$F' > 0, \tag{1.17a}$$

which mean that population is stable when $x = \bar{x}$, and increases (or decreases) when $x > \bar{x}$ (or $x < \bar{x}$).

[29] The function $F$ and the similar function $\Phi$ of the following section are supposed to be continuously differentiable.

The differential equation ($I.17$), with the properties ($I.17a$), is of a type which has been extensively studied by Professor Samuelson in connection with what he calls the *correspondence principle* between comparative statics and dynamics.[30] In our case, it can be easily demonstrated[31] that the dynamic movement for $x(t)$ generated by ($I.17$) is convergent towards $\bar{x}$ (the natural wage-rate), provided that $(dx/dN) < 0$, a condition which the system fulfils.[31] Hence, for $x$, only the *natural* solution $x = \bar{x}$ is a stable solution.

## 7. *The equilibrium of the stationary state*

The *natural* equilibrium examined in the previous sections is still not a stable state of affairs. Two other types of change are in operation in a Ricardian system as time goes on: (i) the improvements which take place in the technical conditions of production – in our terms, the shifts in time of the production function $f(N_1)$ – , and (ii) the accumulation of capital by the capitalists, who add each year a substantial part of their profits to capital. Here again, Ricardo does not consider the first type of change – technical progress – in a systematic way. He only points out that improvements in the technical conditions postpone in time the effects of the changes of type (ii). Since he thinks that these changes (capital accumulation) are – in order of magnitude – the more relevant ones, he concentrates his analysis on them, with the qualification that the effects he shows might be delayed, though not modified, by technical progress.

In analytical terms, capital accumulation represents another dynamic mechanism, in operation on the system already described, of the following type:

$$\frac{dK}{dt} = \Phi\left(\frac{1}{p_1}\pi\right),\qquad (I.18)$$

or, from ($I.8a$) and ($I.11a$),

$$\frac{dK}{dt} = \Phi\left(N[f'(N_1) - x]\right),\qquad (I.19)$$

---

[30] P. A. Samuelson, 'The Stability of Equilibrium: Comparative Statics and Dynamics', *Econometrica*, April 1941, also *Foundations of Economic Analysis*, Cambridge, Mass., 1948, especially chapter IX.

[31] A proof is given in the appendix.

with the properties:[32]

$$\Phi(0) = 0,$$
$$\Phi' > 0. \tag{1.19a}$$

The differential equation (1.19) is of the same type as (1.17) and has now to be considered jointly with it. From mere inspection of the two equations, it can be seen that the solutions of the system at which the two dynamic mechanisms cease to operate (the stationary solutions) emerge when $x = \bar{x}$ and $\pi = 0$. Therefore, for any given state of technical knowledge, represented by the technical function $f(N_1)$, the stationary equilibrium is given by equations (1.1)–(1.14) plus the following two:

$$x = \bar{x} > 0, \tag{1.15}$$

$$\pi = 0. \tag{1.16a}$$

In order to ensure the existence of non-negative solutions for this system, a somewhat stronger condition than (1.1b) is required, namely:

$$f'(0) > \bar{x} > f'(\infty), \tag{1.20}$$

where: $f'(\infty) = \lim_{N_1 \to \infty} f'(N_1)$.

The meaning is that there must be a certain point, as population increases, at which the product of the last worker put to work descends below the *natural* wage-rate (a condition which is implicit in Ricardo's arguments). If this condition were not satisfied, the system would expand indefinitely and the stationary state would never be reached. When (1.20) is satisfied, it is shown in the appendix that two types of solutions exist – one of them corresponds to the equality $f'(N_1) = \bar{x}$ and the other to the equality $N = 0$. The solutions of the second type, however, so called *trivial* (they mean that there is no economic system at all) are uninteresting, and moreover they are *unstable*. On the other hand, the solutions corresponding to $f'(N_1) = \bar{x}$ are unique and perfectly *stable*. Therefore, the system necessarily converges towards them. When the situation they represent is attained, all dynamic mechanisms come to a standstill. The wage-rate is at its natural level (no longer disturbed

---

[32] If a minimum rate of profit (let us call it $\bar{r}$) is considered necessary in order to induce capital accumulation, equation (1.18) has to be modified as follows:
$\dfrac{\mathrm{d}K}{\mathrm{d}t} = \Phi\left(\dfrac{1}{p_1}\pi - \bar{r}K\right)$. However, the conclusions drawn in the text remain the same, with the single modification that the stationary and stable point of convergency of the system, instead of being at $\pi = 0$, is at $\pi = \bar{r}p_1 K$.

by capital accumulation), and the rate of profit has fallen to zero. The system has reached a stable equilibrium – the Ricardian equilibrium of the stationary state.

## 8. *The process of economic growth*

It has been shown in the foregoing sections that the Ricardian system contains many dynamic processes, although some of them are not systematically analysed. The two dynamic processes which are explicitly taken into consideration are convergent and lead to a stationary and stable state. Ricardo, however, investigates the properties of his system at a very particular stage of the whole movement, which he considers the relevant one. Most of his analysis is carried on *as if* the demographic mechanism has already fully worked through, while the capital accumulation process has not yet been completed. In other words, he concentrates on describing the changing characteristics of his system in terms of the *natural* behaviour of the variables in a process of capital accumulation.

In mathematical notation, this task becomes very easy. It is enough to consider the system (1.1)–(1.16) (in which the *natural* wage-rate has been permanently achieved) and to take the derivatives of each variable with respect to capital, which represents the datum – in the *natural* equilibrium – the variation of which in time brings about economic growth. A substantial part of the Ricardian analysis is simply expressed by the signs of these derivatives. Let us consider them:

$$\frac{dN}{dK} = \frac{1}{\bar{x}} > 0, \tag{1.21}$$

$$\frac{dN_1}{dK} = \frac{1}{\bar{x}} \left\{ 1 - \frac{f(N_1) f''(N_1)}{[f'(N_1)]^2} \right\}^{-1} > 0, \tag{1.22}$$

$$\frac{dN_2}{dK} = \frac{1}{\bar{x}} \left\{ 1 - \frac{[f'(N_1)]^2}{f(N_1) f''(N_1)} \right\}^{-1} > 0, \tag{1.23}$$

$$\frac{dX_1}{dK} = f'(N_1) \cdot \frac{dN_1}{dK} > 0, \tag{1.24}$$

$$\frac{dX_2}{dK} = \alpha \frac{dN_2}{dK} > 0, \tag{1.25}$$

$$\frac{dW}{dK} = 1 > 0, \tag{1.26}$$

$$\frac{dR}{dK} = -N_1 \cdot f''(N_1) \cdot \frac{dN_1}{dK} > 0, \tag{1.27}$$

$$\frac{dp_1}{dK} = \frac{-f''(N_1)}{[f'(N_1)]^2} \cdot \frac{dN_1}{dK} > 0, \tag{1.28}$$

$$\frac{dp_2}{dK} = 0, \tag{1.29}$$

$$\frac{dw}{dK} = \bar{x} \cdot \frac{dp_1}{dK} > 0, \tag{1.30}$$

$$\frac{dr}{dK} = \frac{f''(N_1)}{\bar{x}} \cdot \frac{dN_1}{dK} < 0. \tag{1.31}$$

These derivatives have been obtained from the system (1.1)–(1.16) and the inequality signs follow from (1.1$b$), (1.1$c$), (1.15), (1.16), and from other previous inequalities among the (1.21)–(1.31) themselves. Their economic meaning may be stated as follows. The number of workers (employment), all physical productions, the total wage-bill, total rent, the price of corn and the natural *money* wage-rate – all these increase as long as the process of capital accumulation is going on. As an effect of the same process, the rate of profit continually decreases. For Ricardo, it took, of course, a much longer process to show what here is demonstrated merely by the sign of a derivative.

Another variable whose response to capital accumulation particularly requires a long analysis in the *Principles*[33] is total profit. For this variable too, let us consider its derivative with respect to capital. From (1.11$a$) we obtain:

$$\frac{d\pi}{dK} = \frac{1}{f'(N_1)} \left[ \frac{f'(N_1)}{\bar{x}} - 1 + K \cdot \frac{f''(N_1)}{f'(N_1)} \cdot \frac{dN_1}{dK} \right]. \tag{1.32}$$

Now, from (1.1$c$) and (1.22), $f''(N_1) < 0$ and $(dN_1/dK) > 0$. Moreover $f'(N_1) > \bar{x}$, as long as the stationary state has not yet been attained. (At the stationary state $f'(N_1) = \bar{x}$.) Therefore, the sign of (1.32), unlike all the others, is not independent of the amount of $K$. At the beginning of the process of capital accumulation, where $K = 0$, the third term into brackets vanishes and therefore $(d\pi/dK) > 0$. At the stationary state, where $f'(N_1) = \bar{x}$, the first two terms into brackets cancel out, and the

---

[33] *Principles*, chapter VI.

third is negative, so that $(\mathrm{d}\pi/\mathrm{d}K) < 0$. In between, there must be at least one point of maximum total profits, where:

$$\frac{f'(N_1) - \bar{x}}{\bar{x}} = -K \cdot \frac{f''(N_1)}{f'(N_1)} \cdot \frac{\mathrm{d}N_1}{\mathrm{d}K},$$

at which (1.32) changes its sign from positive to negative as capital accumulates.[34] Hence:

$$\frac{\mathrm{d}\pi}{\mathrm{d}K} \gtreqless 0, \quad \text{according as to whether} \quad \frac{f'(N_1)}{\bar{x}} - 1 \gtreqless -K \cdot \frac{f''(N_1)}{f'(N_1)} \cdot \frac{\mathrm{d}N_1}{\mathrm{d}K},$$

which may also be written $\dfrac{f'(N_1)}{\bar{x}} - 1 \gtreqless -\dfrac{E[f'(N_1)]}{E\,K}$,

where the first member of the inequality represents the rate of profit (see equation (1.14a)) and the second member represents the *elasticity* of the marginal product from land with respect to capital.

Analytically, the possibility cannot be excluded of more than one point of maximum, in the sense that $\pi$ might alternatively increase and decrease many times as capital accumulates. For such a possibility to realize, however, the third derivative of $f(N_1)$ must behave in a very peculiar way. Ricardo, of course, did not consider these complications; he explained the process by a long numerical example, which allowed him to consider only the normal case in which, as capital accumulation goes on, total profits increase up to a certain point and then decrease.[35, 36]

[34] The reader may easily verify that, as capital accumulates, profits in sector 1 and in sector 2 (namely the variables $P_1$ and $P_2$) behave exactly in the same way as total profit ($\pi$).

[35] *Principles*, pp. 110 and ff.

[36] In a recent paper by H. Barkai, a very simplified one-commodity Ricardian model is worked out in mathematical terms in order to analyse the movements of *relative shares* as capital accumulates (H. Barkai, 'Ricardo on Factor Prices and Income Distribution in a Growing Economy', *Economica*, August 1959). Dr Barkai uses a procedure which has some similarities with the one I have adopted in this section, but arrives at a curious conclusion. He shows that the relative share of total wages in total product increases as an effect of capital accumulation (which is obvious, as the real wage-rate is constant and the production function is at diminishing returns), and then claims that this result contradicts what Ricardo says on page 112 of his *Principles*, namely that as capital accumulates, 'the labourer's ... real share will be diminished' (Barkai's quotation). But this is a misunderstanding. Dr Barkai's proof refers to the *relative share of total wages* in total product, while Ricardo is talking about the single *labourer's real share*, which is evidently a different thing.

This is a case, incidentally, which illustrates rather well how easy it is to be misled by particular passages in Ricardo's writings. Let me recall the advice of Alfred Marshall: 'If we seek to understand him [Ricardo] rightly, we must interpret him

## 9. *Multi-commodity production*

We are now in a position to drop the two-commodity assumption and extend the system of equations to the general case of multi-commodity production. As far as the wage-goods are concerned, the extension does not present particular difficulties, although it does emphasise the crudeness of Ricardo's assumptions. The economic theory of demand had not yet been developed, at that time, and there is no question of substitution among wage-goods in the Ricardian model. The *natural* wage-rate is represented by a fixed *basket of goods*, to be accepted as given by factors lying outside economic investigation. With this specification, the introduction in our system of any wage-good $i$, besides corn, introduces 8 more variables: $X_i, N_i, W_i, R_i, P_i, K_i, p_i, x_i$, but also 8 more equations of the types (1.1), (1.4), (1.5), (1.6), (1.7), (1.8), (1.15), (1.16). The system is again determinate and maintains its basic features already analysed in the previous sections. In fact, when the *natural* wage-rate is accepted as a fixed basket of goods, there is no gain at all, from an analytical point of view, in extending the system to include any number of wage-goods more than one. The whole structural character of the model is already given by the system of equations (1.1)–(1.16), provided that our interpretation of the single wage-commodity is modified in the sense of considering it as a composite commodity, made up of a fixed mixture of wage-goods.[37] The dynamic characteristics of the model

---

generously, more generously than he himself interpreted Adam Smith. When his words are ambiguous, we must give them that interpretation which other passages in his writings indicate that he would have wished us to give them. If we do this with the desire to ascertain what he really meant, his doctrines, though far from complete, are free from many of the errors that are commonly attributed to them.' (Alfred Marshall, *Principles of Economics*, 8th ed., London 1920, p. 813.)

[37] Professor Samuelson, in his 'Modern Treatment of the Ricardian Economy', *The Quarterly Journal of Economics*, February and May 1959, has been unable to reproduce these properties of the Ricardian model. The reason seems to me that he has treated a Ricardian economy with a production function of the neo-classical type (see especially his appendix), which is inappropriate and is responsible for the conclusions he then criticizes. Professor Samuelson argues that the classification of lands in order of fertility – namely, in our terms, the technical function $f(N_1)$ – is not an unambiguously determined one because, according to the type of produce which is considered, the classification, i.e. the function $f(N_1)$, may be different. This argument is valid in a neo-classical theoretical framework, where substitution among goods (in consumption and in production) is the main feature of the theory, but is irrelevant in a Ricardian type of analysis, which excludes substitution. When the proportion of the different produces is fixed, the classification of lands in order of fertility is a perfectly determined one.

also remain unchanged as they depend exclusively on the wage-goods part of the economy.

The problem becomes much more complicated when the extension to multi-commodity production is made for luxury-goods. Here, the introduction of each commodity $l_j$, besides the one which is used as a standard, introduces 4 more variables: $X_{lj}$, $N_{lj}$, $p_{lj}$, $P_{lj}$, but only 3 more equations of the types (1.2), (1.9) and (1.10). Moreover, it changes equation (1.12) into the following one:

$$p_{l1}X_{l1} + p_{l2}X_{l2} + \ldots p_{lj}X_{lj} + \ldots p_{ln}X_{ln} = p_wR, \qquad (1.12a)$$

where the subscript $w$ stands for the composite wage-commodity and the subscripts $l_j$'s stand for the luxury-goods.

Hence, for each luxury-commodity introduced besides the first, one more relation is needed in order to keep the system determinate. Ricardo *does not* provide this relation. Again the difficulty is that he does not have a theory of demand. The assumption of a natural wage-rate solves the problem for the workers (and by consequence for the capitalists) but leaves it still open for the landlords, whose possibilities of substituting one luxury-good for another and whose changes of tastes cannot be ruled out; and Ricardo does not rule them out. Have we to conclude, therefore, that the Ricardian system is indeterminate with respect to the luxury-goods? It certainly is, but – interestingly enough – only for the particular variables $X_{lj}$'s, $N_{lj}$'s, $P_{lj}$'s, which are not really of much interest to an economist like Ricardo, *once their totals are determined*.

To see this surprising property of the Ricardian system, let us suppose that $n$ luxury-goods are produced. Then $4(n-1)$ new variables of the types $X_{lj}$, $N_{lj}$, $P_{lj}$, $p_{lj}$, and $3(n-1)$ new equations of the types (1.2), (1.9) and (1.10) are introduced in the already analysed system. Provisionally, let us write down $n$ demand equations for the luxury goods:

$$\begin{aligned}
X_{l1} &= \varphi_1(p_w, p_{l1}, p_{l2}, \ldots \ldots p_{ln}, R), \\
X_{l2} &= \varphi_2(p_w, p_{l1}, p_{l2}, \ldots \ldots p_{ln}, R), \\
&\quad \cdot \\
&\quad \cdot \\
&\quad \cdot \\
X_{ln} &= \varphi_n(p_w, p_{l1}, p_{l2}, \ldots \ldots p_{ln}, R).
\end{aligned} \qquad (1.33)$$

Equation (1.12a), which represents Say's law (namely, landlords spend all their income – no more and no less – on luxury-goods), puts a restriction on the (1.33), so that one of the equations may be dropped.

19

We are left with $(n-1)$ equations, which is the number necessary to determine the system. It is very interesting to notice now that the solutions for all the variables of the system, except the $X_{lj}$'s, $P_{lj}$'s, $N_{lj}$'s, are independent of the (1.33). In other words, the (1.33) are only required to determine physical production, employment and profits in each particular luxury-good sector, but are not required to determine all the other variables. *Whatever the demand equations for luxury-goods may be*, i.e., independently of them, all the variables referring to the wage-goods part of the economy, all prices, the rate of profit, and all the macro-economic variables of the system – like total employment, national income, total profits, total rent, total wages, total capital – are already determined by the system.

This is perhaps the most interesting outcome of the whole mathematical formulation attempted in this essay and it will be useful to remind the reader of the assumptions under which it has been reached: (i) perfect mobility of capital; (ii) Say's Law; (iii) the assumption of circulating capital only, and of a one-year period for *all* processes of production. The last assumption, so stated, is too restrictive. As a matter of fact, it may be dropped and fixed capital introduced into the analysis without affecting the already attained conclusions, *provided that* the somewhat more general restriction is kept of supposing that all the sectors of the economy use fixed and circulating capital of the same durability and in the same proportions. *This is indeed the crucial assumption* – the determinateness of the whole Ricardian system itself depends on it, in an essential way.

Ricardo became aware of this limitation of his theoretical model in connection with the problem of the determination of total employment in the economy. He was disturbed by the discovery and, as a result, in the third edition of the *Principles*, he added the well-known chapter 'on machinery'. The problem is that, when the mentioned crucial assumption holds, total employment in the economy, for any given amount of capital, is determined independently of the (1.33). But when the conditions of the assumption are not realized, total employment comes out different according to the way in which demand (and therefore capital) is distributed among the luxury-goods sectors. Having realized this, Ricardo candidly admitted, in the added chapter, that he was mistaken earlier, when he extended to the introduction of machinery (i.e., to the case where the proportions of fixed and circulating capital change) his general conclusions about total employment depending on total capital alone and not on how and where this capital is employed. This proposition, in the light of our formulation, appears quite obvious, but it has not appeared so to many of Ricardo's interpreters. Indeed because of the assertions it contains, which seem to be in contradiction with the general conclusions following from the whole previous analysis, the chapter 'on machinery' has always puzzled Ricardo's readers. The mathematical formulation of the present essay helps to clarify the issue. It shows that the Ricardian model stands on the assumption of a uniform composition of capital all over the economy. The problem of introduction of machinery exactly hypothesizes a violation of this assumption. Therefore, the general conclusions cannot be extended to this case. Looked at in these terms, the chapter 'on machinery' appears, rather than a contradiction, an honest acknowledgement by Ricardo of the limitations of his theory.

## 10. *Concluding remarks*

A few remarks may be made by way of conclusion.

Ricardo's model is built on very crude assumptions. The most crucial of them is that all sectors of the economy use – we might say in more modern terms – the same period of production. This was just the point against which his contemporary critics (especially Malthus) directed their most violent attacks. In their function as critics, they were right. The limits entailed by the assumption are relevant not only for the Ricardian theory of value – as has always been thought – but also for the determinateness itself of the whole system, as soon as the simple case of two-commodity production is departed from.

On the other hand, once the assumptions underlying the whole analysis have been explicitly defined, the system appears to be logically consistent and determinate in all its macro-economic features and even in its sectoral details, except for some particular sectoral variables in which Ricardo was not interested. A mathematical formulation of the model is possible, clarifies many issues – among others, those connected with the controversial chapter 'on machinery' – and permits a representation of the Ricardian dynamic processes – in particular the process of economic growth – in a rigorous and concise notation. The solutions of the *natural* system Ricardo was dealing with are shown to exist and to be unique but not stable. They reach a perfect stability only in the equilibrium of the stationary state.

The whole model, in its crudeness and simplicity, appears remarkably complete and synthetic. Ricardo is always looking for fundamentals. Detailed relations are dealt with only in the light of basic tendencies – when they become too complicated and lead to difficulties, those relations which are thought to be less important are *frozen* by crude assumptions. Whether this is a fruitful methodological line to pursue is open to controversy. Later, neo-classical economists preferred a radically different line of approach. They abandoned too ambitious dynamic outlooks and started instead to analyse, in a complete way and in all its functional interrelationships, a more simplified (static) version of economic reality. The step which was supposed to follow, however, – that of passing to a dynamic analysis – has not come out as easy and spontaneous as was expected, and, in recent years, it has not been infrequent for economists, faced with urgent problems of economic development, to have second thoughts on the subject. In this light, the Ricardian analysis, with all the *naïveté* and the limits of its particular theories, appears less primitive now-a-days than it appeared some decades ago.

## *APPENDIX*

### *Existence and uniqueness of stable solutions*

It has been a widespread concern among mathematical economists in the last few decades not to be satisfied any longer (as economists used to be) with mere counting the number of equations and unknowns of their theoretical systems and to enquire more rigorously into the conditions for the existence, uniqueness and stability of the solutions. The task has not proved to be an easy one, as it normally entails mathematical notions and manipulations of a fairly highly sophisticated nature. In our case, fortunately, the proofs can be given in a relatively elementary way, except perhaps for the stability conditions.

1. *Existence and uniqueness of non-negative, non-trivial solutions.* The Ricardian system contains one single *functional* relation, the $f(N_1)$. Therefore, the fundamental step to solving it is to find the value of $N_1$ which satisfies the restrictions put by the system on the $f(N_1)$. In the system (I.1)–(I.15), (I.16a), we may start by taking (I.11a), substitute it into (I.16a), and obtain:

$$N[f'(N_1) - \bar{x}] = 0.$$

This equation is satisfied either by $f'(N_1) = \bar{x}$ or by $N = 0$. The latter solution means that there is no economic system at all. Any theoretical representation of an economic system has this solution, but it is an uninteresting one – it represents the so-called *trivial* case. Evidently, the *relevant* solution is the other one. Let us prove therefore:

  (i) that $N_1^*$ – defined as the solution of the equation $f'(N_1) = \bar{x}$ – exists and is non-negative;

 (ii) that $N_1^*$ is unique; and finally,

(iii) that $f(N_1^*) \geqslant N_1^* f'(N_1^*)$. (The reason for this proof will appear in a moment.)

*Proof* (i). From (1.20), $f'(0)$ exists and is greater than $\bar{x}$; $f'(\infty)$ also exists and is smaller than $\bar{x}$. Since $\bar{x}$ is a positive constant, there must be a value $0 < N_1^* < \infty$, at which $f'(N_1^*) = \bar{x}$. Hence $N_1^*$ exists and is non-negative.

*Proof* (ii). From (1.1c), $f''(N_1) < 0$, namely $f'(N_1)$ is a monotonic function. Since $\bar{x}$ is a constant, then (by a straightforward application of Rolle's theorem) $N_1^*$ is unique.

*Proof* (iii). Call $G = f(N_1) - N_1 f'(N_1)$. Then $(dG/dN_1) = -N_1 f''(N_1) > 0$, namely $G$ is a monotonically increasing function. Since $f(0) \geqslant 0$ and $N_1 \geqslant 0$, from (1.1a) and (i), then $G$ is never negative, or $f(N_1) \geqslant N_1 f'(N_1)$ and, in particular, $f(N_1^*) \geqslant N_1^* f'(N_1^*)$.

By substituting now $N_1^*$ into the system of equations (1.1)–(1.15), (1.16a), the solutions come out as:

$$X_1 = f(N_1^*), \quad \text{(A.1)}; \qquad p_1 = \frac{1}{f'(N_1^*)}, \quad \text{(A.9)}$$

$$X_2 = \alpha \left[ \frac{f(N_1^*)}{f'(N_1^*)} - N_1^* \right], \quad \text{(A.2)}; \qquad p_2 = \frac{1}{\alpha}, \quad \text{(A.10)}$$

$$N = \frac{f(N_1^*)}{f'(N_1^*)}, \quad \text{(A.3)}; \qquad w = \bar{x} \frac{1}{f'(N_1^*)}, \quad \text{(A.11)}$$

$$N_1 = N_1^*, \quad \text{(A.4)}; \qquad P_1 = 0, \quad \text{(A.12)}$$

$$N_2 = \frac{f(N_1^*)}{f'(N_1^*)} - N_1^*, \quad \text{(A.5)}; \qquad P_2 = 0, \quad \text{(A.13)}$$

$$W = \bar{x} \frac{f(N_1^*)}{f'(N_1^*)}, \quad \text{(A.6)}; \qquad r = 0, \quad \text{(A.14)}$$

$$K = \bar{x} \frac{f(N_1^*)}{f'(N_1^*)}, \quad \text{(A.7)}; \qquad x = \bar{x}, \quad \text{(A.15)}$$

$$R = f(N_1^*) - N_1^* f'(N_1^*), \quad \text{(A.8)}; \qquad \pi = 0. \quad \text{(A.16)}$$

It follows that, if $N_1^*$ exists, is unique and non-negative and, moreover, if $f(N_1^*) \geqslant N_1^* f'(N_1^*)$, then all (A.1)–(A.16), namely the non-trivial solutions of the system, exist, are unique and are non-negative. The proofs have been given so far with reference to the equations (I.1)–(I.15), (I.16a). *A fortiori*, the solutions of any other system of equations (I.1)–(I.16), defined by a given $\bar{K}$ between 0 and $K^*$, exist, are unique and non-negative. For the system (I.1)–(I.16) the trivial solutions are even excluded by hypothesis as $\bar{K} > 0$. (The stars * are taken to denote the non-trivial solutions of the stationary equilibrium.)

2. *The stability of the stationary equilibrium.* The stationary equilibrium is defined by the solutions of the system of equations (I.1)–(I.15), (I.16a). In order to find out whether it is stable, an investigation has to be made into the dynamic behaviour of the system when *displaced* from the equilibrium solutions. That behaviour is represented by the two differential equations (I.17) and (I.18). For a rigorous proof of stability, the two equations have to be considered jointly. Such a proof is given below but, as it entails a rather sophisticated mathematical treatment, it may be useful to give first a more simple proof which, although less rigorous, is intuitively easier to grasp and is perhaps also more pertinent to the Ricardian logic.

The function (I.17) depends on the deviation of $x$ from $\bar{x}$ and the function (I.18) on the deviation of $f'(N_1)$ from $x$. The two dynamic mechanisms are, so to speak, one on the top of the other. We may begin, therefore, by proving first, for a given $\bar{K}$; the convergency of the first dynamic process towards $\bar{x}$ and then substitute this stable solution into the second process and carry on a similar investigation on it, for a given $\bar{x}$.

Let us take equation (I.17) and expand it in a Taylor series around a value of $N$ defined as $N^+ = \bar{K}/\bar{x}$ :

$$\frac{\mathrm{d}(N - N^+)}{\mathrm{d}t} = F(0) + (N - N^+)F'(0)\frac{\mathrm{d}x}{\mathrm{d}N}$$

$$+ \frac{(N - N^+)^2}{2}\left[ F''(0)\left(\frac{\mathrm{d}x}{\mathrm{d}N}\right)^2 + F'(0)\frac{\mathrm{d}^2x}{\mathrm{d}N^2}\right] + \cdots$$

Neglecting the terms of higher order than the first and recalling that $F(0) = 0$, the equation becomes:

$$\frac{\mathrm{d}(N - N^+)}{\mathrm{d}t} = (N - N^+)\cdot F'(0) \cdot \frac{\mathrm{d}x}{\mathrm{d}N}.$$

This is a simple differential equation and its solution is[38]:

$$N(t) = N^+ + [N(0) - N^+] \cdot \exp\left[F'(0) \cdot \frac{dx}{dN} \cdot t\right],$$

where: $N(0)$ is the value of $N$ at time zero.

Since $F'(0) > 0$ from (1.17a), a necessary condition for $N(t)$ to converge towards $N^+$ (and therefore for $x(t)$ to converge towards $\bar{x}$) is $(dx/dN) < 0$. Now, from the system (1.1)–(1.14), (1.15a), (1.16), we have $(dx/dN) = -(\bar{K}/N^2) < 0$. *The condition is fulfilled.* Hence, *the solution $x = \bar{x}$ is stable.*

By substituting now $x = \bar{x}$ into (1.19) and developing the same type of analysis, the necessary condition for $K$ to converge towards $K^*$ – defined as the stationary equilibrium solution for $K$ – is:

$$\frac{d}{dK}\left(\frac{1}{p_1}\pi\right) < 0.$$

Now, from (1.11a) we can write:

$$\frac{d}{dK}\left(\frac{1}{p_1}\pi\right) = \frac{f'(N_1)}{\bar{x}} - 1 + N \cdot f''(N_1)\frac{dN_1}{dK}.$$

Since $f''(N_1)$ is negative and $f'(N_1)$ is greater or equal to $\bar{x}$ according as to whether $N_1 < N_1^*$ or $N_1 = N_1^*$, then condition $d[(1/p_1)\pi]/dK < 0$ is not satisfied when $N = 0$, while it is satisfied when $f'(N_1) = \bar{x}$. Hence, *the solutions of the system corresponding to $f'(N_1) = \bar{x}$ are stable, while the trivial solutions are unstable* – the system necessarily converges towards the first ones. As a conclusion, the system (1.1)–(1.15), (1.16a) has *stable solutions.* Such stable solutions are also *unique.*

3. *A more rigorous proof of stability.* Consider equations (1.17) and (1.18), representing the variations in time of $N$ and of $K$. Since $N_1$ is a monotonically increasing function of $N$, the equations may be equally expressed in terms of $N_1$ (namely in terms of the wage-goods sector):

$$\frac{dN_1}{dt} = g(x - \bar{x}); \quad g(0) = 0; \cdot \quad g' > 0; \tag{A.17}$$

$$\frac{dK_1}{dt} = \varphi(P_1), \quad \text{where} \quad K_1 = N_1 x; \quad \varphi(0) = 0; \quad \varphi' > 0. \tag{A.18}$$

Our purpose is now to investigate the dynamic behaviour of the system in the vicinity of the stationary solutions $x = \bar{x}$ and $f'(N_1) = x$. Let us

---

[38] See any elementary treatise on differential equations.

expand (A.17) in a Taylor series around the value $\bar{x}$. Neglecting the terms of higher order than the first the equation may be written:

$$\frac{d(N_1 - N_1^*)}{dt} = (x - \bar{x})\, g'(0). \tag{A.17a}$$

Equation (A.18) is more complex. Let us first write it in terms of the same variables entering (A.17):

$$\frac{dK_1}{dt} = \frac{d(N_1\, x)}{dt} = \varphi(N_1[f'(N_1) - x]).$$

By expanding also this equation in a Taylor series and neglecting the terms of higher order than the first we obtain:

$$N_1 \frac{dx}{dt} + x\, \frac{dN_1}{dt} = \varphi'(0) \cdot \{N_1[f'(N_1) - x]\}. \tag{A.19}$$

Let us now express the variables in terms of deviations from their stationary solutions and utilize Taylor's theorem for the $f'(N_1)$. We have:

$$[N_1^* + (N_1 - N_1^*)]\, \frac{d(x - \bar{x})}{dt} + [\bar{x} + (x - \bar{x})]\, \frac{d(N_1 - N_1^*)}{dt}$$
$$= \varphi'(0) \cdot \{[N_1^* + (N_1 - N_1^*)] \cdot [(N_1 - N_1^*) \cdot f''(N_1^*)$$
$$- x + f'(N_1^*)]\}.$$

The squares of $(N_1 - N_1^*)$ and of $(x - \bar{x})$, and their products, represent magnitudes of second order and we may neglect them, rewriting the whole expression as:

$$N_1^* \frac{d(x - \bar{x})}{dt} + \bar{x}\, \frac{d(N_1 - N_1^*)}{dt}$$
$$= \varphi'(0) \cdot N_1^* \cdot [(N_1 - N_1^*) \cdot f''(N_1^*) - x + \bar{x}]$$
$$+ 0\, \{(x - \bar{x})^2;\, (N_1 - N_1^*)^2;\, (x - \bar{x})(N_1 - N_1^*)\}, \tag{A.20}$$

where the last term denotes the order of magnitude of the neglected products. Multiplying now (A.17a) by $\bar{x}$ and subtracting it from (A.20), we can at last write down our equations in a suitable form for an immediate solution:

26

$$\frac{d(N_1 - N_1^*)}{dt} = (x - \bar{x}) \cdot g'(0) + 0\,\{(x - \bar{x})^2\},$$

$$\frac{d(x - \bar{x})}{dt} = (N_1 - N_1^*) \cdot \varphi'(0) \cdot f''(N_1^*)$$

$$- (x - \bar{x}) \cdot \left\{\frac{\bar{x}}{N_1^*}\, g'(0) + \varphi'(0)\right\}$$

$$+ 0\,\{(x - \bar{x})^2; (N_1 - N_1^*)^2; (x - \bar{x})(N_1 - N_1^*)\}.$$

The solutions of this system of equations – apart from the neglected terms – take the form[39]:

$$N_1(t) = N_1^* + k_{11} \exp(\lambda_1 t) + k_{12} \exp(\lambda_2 t),$$

$$x(t) = \bar{x} + k_{21} \exp(\lambda_1 t) + k_{22} \exp(\lambda_2 t),$$

where the $k$'s depend on the values of $N_1$ and $x$ at time zero and the $\lambda$'s are the roots of the characteristic equation:

$$\begin{vmatrix} 0 - \lambda & g'(0) \\ \varphi'(0) \cdot f''(N_1^*) & -\dfrac{\bar{x}}{N_1^*}\, g'(0) - \varphi'(0) - \lambda \end{vmatrix} = 0,$$

or:

$$\lambda^2 + \lambda\left[\varphi'(0) + \frac{\bar{x}}{N_1^*} \cdot g'(0)\right] - g'(0) \cdot \varphi'(0) \cdot f''(N_1^*) = 0. \quad \text{(A.21)}$$

For the equilibrium to be stable the real part of $\lambda$ must be necessarily negative, i.e.,

$$R(\lambda) < 0. \tag{A.22}$$

Now, since $\varphi'(0) > 0$, $g'(0) > 0$, and $f''(N_1) < 0$, (A.21) can be written as:

$$\lambda^2 + 2\,m\lambda + n^2 = 0, \tag{A.23}$$

where:

$$m = \tfrac{1}{2}[\varphi'(0) + \frac{\bar{x}}{N_1}\, g'(0)]; \qquad n = \sqrt{[-\,g'(0) \cdot \varphi'(0) \cdot f''(N_1^*)]}.$$

[39] See, for example, A. R. Forsyth, *A Treatise on Differential Equations*, London, 1921, pp. 342 and ff.

Hence:

$$\lambda = -m \pm (m^2 - n^2)^{\frac{1}{2}},$$

from which it appears that the real part of $\lambda$ is always negative, namely that condition (A.22) is satisfied. Therefore, the *stationary equilibrium defined by the couple of solutions* $x = \bar{x}$ *and* $f'(N_1) = \bar{x}$ *is stable.*

A proof of the instability of the trivial solutions, characterized by $N_1 = 0$, can be given in an easier way because in this case the products involving $N_1$ itself – besides those involving $(x - \bar{x})$ – are of second order of smallness and equation (A.18) may be considered in isolation, as appears by rewriting (A.19) as:

$$N_1 \frac{d(x - \bar{x})}{dt} + (x - \bar{x} + \bar{x}) \frac{dN_1}{dt} = \varphi'(0) N_1[f'(0) - x + \bar{x} - \bar{x}],$$

and then, neglecting the squares of $N_1$ and of $(x - \bar{x})$ and their products:

$$\frac{1}{N_1} \frac{dN_1}{dt} = \frac{1}{\bar{x}} \varphi'(0) [f'(0) - \bar{x}] + 0 \{N_1{}^2; (x - \bar{x})^2; N_1(x - \bar{x})\}.$$

This is a simple differential equation the solution of which – apart from the neglected terms – takes the form:

$$\log_n N_1 = kt + \log_n C, \tag{A.24}$$

namely:

$$N_1(t) = C \exp (kt), \tag{A.25}$$

where: $k = \dfrac{1}{\bar{x}} \varphi'(0) [f'(0) - \bar{x}]$,      and $C = N_1(0)$.

Since $(1/\bar{x}) \varphi'(0)[f'(0) - \bar{x}] > 0$, then the solution (A.25) is explosive, which means that *the stationary equilibrium defined by the solution* $N_1 = 0$ *is unstable.*

# II

# The economics of effective demand

It is not difficult, at a century and a half's distance, to see the many deficiencies of Ricardo's theory. Even leaving aside all the problems connected with his theory of value,[1] there are three major shortcomings that cry out for correction: Ricardo's naïve view of population growth, his under-estimation of technical progress, and his inability to grasp the importance of effective demand.

In the present essay attention will be concentrated on effective demand, the role of which has become clear to us only after the publication of Keynes' *General Theory*. Keynes himself explicitly linked up his analysis of effective demand with a long discussion that took place between Ricardo and Malthus.[2] A few words on this famous discussion may be helpful.

## 1. *Malthus on effective demand*

Malthus' *Principles of Political Economy Considered with a View to their Practical Applications* appeared in 1820 as an answer to Ricardo. Among the views that Malthus attacked was the traditional one that 'every frugal man is a public benefactor'. He retorted that 'the principle of saving, pushed to excess, would destroy the motive of production'. And he added that 'if production is in great excess above consumption, the motive to accumulate and produce must cease from the want of will to consume'.[3] On this basis, Malthus defended the unproductive consumption of the landlords as a remedy to 'market gluts', and warned

---

[1] These problems have recently attracted new attention after the publication of Piero Sraffa, *Production of Commodities by Means of Commodities*, Cambridge, 1960.

[2] John Maynard Keynes, *The General Theory of Employment Interest and Money*, London 1936, chapter 23; and 'Thomas Robert Malthus', in *Essays in Biography*, London, 1933.

[3] T. R. Malthus, *Principles of Political Economy Considered with a View to their Practical Application*, London, 1820, pp. 8–9.

against the dire consequences of excessive 'parsimony and thrift'. He devoted ample space to the problem, and summarized it as the 'questions, 1st whether the motive to accumulate may be checked from the want of demand, before it is checked by the difficulty of procuring food; and 2ndly, whether such check is probable'. His answers to both questions were positive. And the prescription followed consequentially: 'we may conclude that a body of unproductive labourers is necessary as a stimulus to wealth'.[4]

Ricardo failed to see any force in these arguments. For him, savings were associated with the capitalists and therefore meant the same thing as capital accumulation. It was, moreover, very easy for him to appeal to the authority of the leading French economist of the time, Jean-Baptiste Say, who had stated that any production generates its own demand – what has then become universally known as *la loi des débouchés* or 'Say's Law'.[5] Unfortunately, Malthus' replies remained ineffective. Malthus lacked the minimum analytical tools necessary to give expression to his contention. He even failed to stress effectively what was absolutely necessary to his arguments, namely the distinction between the savings of the landlords and the capital accumulation of the capitalists.[6]

[4] These are Malthus' own summary words for his pp. 478–9; *Ibid.* p. 587. Most of Malthus' arguments on the importance of effective demand are contained in section IX of chapter VII of his *Principles*, and restated in a series of letters to Ricardo. (See, as an example, letter 7 July 1821, in vol. IX pp. 9–11 of *The Works and Correspondence of David Ricardo*, ed. by Piero Sraffa.)

[5] 'Say's Law' is enunciated in a few short passages in the chapter 'Des débouchés' (book I) of his *Traité d'économic politique* (1st ed. 1803). We find there the famous passage: 'It is worth while to remark that a product is no sooner created, than it, from that instant, affords a market for other products to the full extent of its own value. When the producer has put the finishing hand to his product, he is most anxious to sell it immediately, lest its value should vanish in his hands. Nor is he less anxious to dispose of the money he may get for it; for the value of money is also perishable. But the only way of getting rid of money is in the purchase of some product or other. Thus, the mere circumstance of the creation of one product immediately opens a vent (*un débouché*) for other products.' (From the English translation of the fourth French edition: Jean-Baptiste Say, *A Treatise of Political Economy*, London, 1821, vol. I, p. 167.)

[6] This failure of Malthus to stress that his arguments applied to the thrift and savings of 'those classes that do not produce' has recently induced some critics to deny him the role of precursor of Keynes. (See, for example, B. A. Corry, 'Malthus and Keynes – a Reconsideration', *The Economic Journal*, 1959, pp. 717–24; P. Garegnani, 'Note su consumi, investimenti e domanda effettiva', parte prima, *Economia Internazionale*, 1964, pp. 591–631.) But it seems to me that this is going too far. The fact that Malthus was analytically weak and that he was not always logically consistent may explain why he was not successful; but cannot take away from him the merit of having been aware precisely of those problems of lack of effective demand, which Keynes was able to deal with, in a theoretically better and successful way, a century later.

The controversy dragged on, and died out in the end in a sterile dispute on how long in time was the term under discussion.[7] Ricardo and Malthus remained, of course, of their original opinion; but it was the analytically stronger Ricardian theories that carried the professional opinion. And it was of no avail for Malthus to appeal to the factual evidence of common experience and to stress the *practical* importance of the theory (explicit reference to 'practical applications' is made in the very title of his book[8]). Stronger theory prevailed.

A century later, at the peak of his enthusiasm for Malthus, Keynes could exclaim: 'If only Malthus, instead of Ricardo, had been the parent stem from which nineteenth-century economics proceeded, what a much wiser and richer place the world would be today!'[9]. But Keynes' hypothetical wish was illusory. Malthus' weak arguments on effective demand could never have carried the burden of nineteenth-century economic theory. What would have been necessary was a logically consistent theory that could embody and express Malthus' intuitive ideas. This we could get only from Keynes a century later.

## 2. *The principle of effective demand*

The basic principle which has remained hidden for so long and which may be called 'the principle of effective demand' can be stated straight-away in a very concise form.

Among the peculiarities which an industrial society has acquired, with respect to more primitive (agricultural) societies, there is one that requires us to make a sharp distinction between productive capacity and actual production. In primitive (agricultural) societies, each farmer tries to produce as much as he can. He will then take whatever amount of his produce is in excess of his needs to the market. And there this produce will fetch the price the market makes. In an industrial society it is not so. At any given point of time, productive capacity is indeed what it is – it cannot be changed. But productive capacity does not mean

[7] 'It appears to me that one great cause of our difference in opinion, on the subjects which we have so often discussed, is that you have always in your mind the immediate and temporary effects of particular changes – whereas I put these immediate and temporary effects quite aside, and fix my whole attention on the permanent state of things which will result from them.' (From Ricardo's letter to Malthus, 24 January 1817, in vol VII, p. 120, of *The Works and Correspondence of David Ricardo*, ed. by Piero Sraffa.) Here Malthus would have needed Keynes' knack of repartee: 'in the long run we are all dead!'

[8] See footnote 3 above.

[9] Keynes, *Essays in Biography*, pp. 120–1.

production – it only means *potential* production. In order that there may be *actual* production, there must be *effective demand*.

The point may be expressed with the help of a well-known diagram introduced by Alvin Hansen[10], in which total net production (or net national income $Y$) appears on the abscissa and total effective demand ($D$) on the ordinate, and in which a 45° line is drawn. (See fig. II.1.)

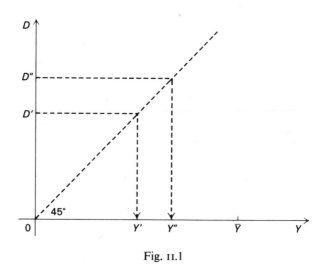

Fig. II.1

Up to the point $\bar{Y}$ – representing full capacity utilization – whatever total demand may be ($D'$ or $D''$), net production will turn out to be precisely the same ($Y'$ or $Y''$). Quite simply: demand generates income. If producers were to expect a fall in demand, they would reduce production accordingly, *quite irrespective* of the level of their productive capacity. And they would do the opposite if they were to expect an increase of demand. Therefore, as long as there is idle capacity to use, fluctuations of demand generate fluctuations of production, while prices will remain more or less unaffected. It is only when demand goes beyond point $\bar{Y}$ – full capacity utilization – that physical production will be constrained at $\bar{Y}$, and that an increase in demand may cause increases in prices (an inflationary movement). The income generation process will, however, go on in the same way as before, with the important

[10] See his *A Guide to Keynes*, New York, 1953, and all his textbooks on Keynesian economics.

difference that the additions to income will only be in monetary terms, since in real terms production cannot exceed productive capacity.[11]

It must be stressed that all this is meant to refer to an industrial society (as against the case of a more primitive agricultural and artisan society, where fluctuations of demand normally determine fluctuations of prices, at the given amount of production). What this typical behaviour of an industrial economic system depends on is a question which would take too long to go into here, and has not even been completely and successfully investigated so far by the economists themselves. Many factors may be mentioned, all acting in a cumulative way: stickiness of prices due to oligopolistic situations, mark-up pricing rules in manufacturing business, contractually fixed wage-rates, etc., and many other factors which are continually evolving. The basic feature remains, by contrast with more primitive societies, that among the factors concurring to determining prices, fluctuations of demand have become unimportant. Therefore, the traditional response mechanism of price changes having become inoperative, another response mechanism is brought into use. To changes in demand, producers respond by changing production.

This has a very serious consequence. Changes in production entail changes in the utilization of existing productive capacity and in the employment of labour. A fall of total demand generates unemployment and a slump – a bitter reality so often experienced in capitalist economies. There are machines, and there are workers able to man them, but they all remain idle for lack of effective demand.

### 3. *Theories of under-consumption (and over-production)*

The principle of effective demand may appear very simple; so simple in fact as to make one wonder why it has taken so long to emerge. But the plain answer to this is that many authors did perceive it in the past, though they never succeeded in making of it an accepted tenet of official economic theory.

---

[11] This way of presenting the problem is, of course, a simplification. In practice full capacity utilization may be reached at different moments in different sectors. There may be sectors working at full capacity even in a prevailing slump situation, and there may be sectors with idle capacity even when total demand as a whole has out-grown total existing productive capacity. This means that full employment production must not be rigidly taken as coming at a singular point. There may be a band around $Y$, in which fluctuations of demand induce changes in production in some sectors and changes in prices in other sectors. But the proportion of the quantity changes, with respect to the price changes, will be the higher the farther the system is on the left of $\bar{Y}$, and will be the lower the farther the system is on the right of $\bar{Y}$.

The unsuccessful attempts have a long history. At the time of the Ricardo–Malthus discussions, the Swiss-Italian economist, Sismondi, who criticized Ricardo rather violently, had among his major contentions precisely the claim that capitalist systems tend to situations of under-consumption.[12] Later Karl Marx, the sharpest of all critics of capitalism, indicted capitalist societies, among other things, also for over-production – a situation which in his theory is expressed by crises in the 'realization of surplus value'.[13] And at the turn of the century, John Hobson insisted on the existence of under-consumption in capitalist systems in almost all his (numerous) works.[14] Moreover, one may say that practically all the economists who have been concerned with 'crises' and business cycles (e.g. Lauderdale, Tugan-Baranowski, Aftalion, Spiethoff, etc., and again all the Marxists, such as Hilferding, Rosa Luxemburg, Bukharin, etc.) did come, at one stage or another, to stress the possibility and the disastrous consequences of a gap between potential production and effective demand.

Yet, all these authors have had very little success in their times. The attitude of the established economic profession towards them has always been one of great contempt, in the belief that their theories contained all sorts of analytical faults. Under-consumption theories were simply regarded as bad theories. And in fact it must be said that established economic theory made the task of refuting them rather easy. Any well-trained economist could do so with arguments that appeared logically unexceptionable. In the early nineteenth century these arguments would take the form of a simple enunciation of Say's Law; and in the early twentieth century they would take the more sophisticated form of

[12] J. C. L. Simonde de Sismondi, *Nouveaux principes d'économie politique*, Paris, 1819. Unlike Malthus, who criticized Ricardo, so to speak, from the right – in favour of the landlords – Sismondi criticized Ricardo, in a sense, from the left – in favour of the workers. But neither of them was obviously the first to realize the dangers of under-consumption. As Keynes points out in chapter 23 of the *General Theory*, much of the Mercantilists' writings can be given sense if interpreted as preoccupation with a lack of effective demand. There is moreover the famous case of the satirical *Fable of the Bees*, by Bernard Mandeville, a book convicted as scandalous by the grand jury of Middlesex in 1723, for the praise it made of extravagance as a public virtue.

[13] Marx's remarks on effective demand are mainly contained in vol. II of *Das Kapital*, but are also scattered over vols. I and III. For a synthetic account, see: Henry Smith, 'Marx and the Trade Cycle', *The Review of Economic Studies*, 1936–7, pp. 192–204; John D. Wilson, 'A Note on Marx and the Trade Cycle', *ibid.* 1937–8, pp. 107–13. See also: part III, 'Crises and Depressions' of Paul M. Sweezy, *The Theory of Capitalist Development*, New York, 1942; and the chapter on effective demand in Joan Robinson, *An Essay on Marxian Economics*, London, 1942.

[14] See especially his *The Industrial System*, London, 1909, and *Economics of Unemployment*, London, 1922.

a general equilibrium scheme, in which the total available resources are considered as given, and competition determines the (equilibrium) prices, which are such as to lead to the clearance of all markets. It simply sounded inconceivable, to a professional economist, that any resource could remain unused, except for temporary frictions, as long as its price is positive. And it simply sounded inconceivable that there could be a situation of equilibrium with 'involuntary' unemployment.[15]

In Great Britain, the most famous expression of these arguments is contained in a Government official paper, representing 'the Treasury view of 1929'. In that official paper, the economists of the British Treasury – mainly well-trained Oxford and Cambridge economists – opposed the proposal, made by Lloyd George in an election campaign, of public works to alleviate unemployment, with the argument that public works would only cause an *increase* of unemployment. For, the available funds being given, their absorption for public works could only subtract them from other (productive) investments.[16]

This view seems almost incredible today. And yet it was the prevailing professional view only forty years ago. Only in the 1930s did the theoretical scene change radically. The conditions of the time became, of course, favourable to such a change. In 1929–33 the Western industrialized countries went through the most severe and dramatic of all depressions they ever experienced. Two great economists of that time – Kalecki and Keynes – though with entirely different backgrounds (Kalecki in Poland, proceeding from Marx[17], and Keynes in England, rebelling against Marshall), independently arrived at almost the same conclusions on effective demand. It was Keynes however who gained universal success. And there is little doubt – it seems to me – that Keynes' success was due in a decisive manner to the fact that –

[15] Consider the following much quoted passage of Pigou's: 'the state of demand for labour, as distinguished from changes in that state, is irrelevant to unemployment, because wage-rates adjust themselves in such a manner that different states of· demand, when once established, tend to be associated with similar average rates of unemployment ... With perfectly free competition among work-people and labour perfectly mobile ... there will always be ... a strong tendency for wage-rates to be so related to demand [for labour] that everybody is employed. Hence, in stable conditions every one will actually be employed. The implication is that such unemployment as exists at any time is due wholly to the fact that changes in demand conditions are continually taking place and that frictional resistances prevent the appropriate wage adjustments from being made instantaneously.' (A. C. Pigou, *The Theory of Unemployment*, London, 1933, p. 252.)

[16] *Memoranda on Certain Proposals Relating to Unemployment*, Cmd. 3331.

[17] See especially his selection of papers, recently published in English: Michal Kalecki, *Selected Essays on the Dynamics of the Capitalist Economy, 1933–1970*, Cambridge, 1971.

unlike all his under-consumptionist predecessors – he was able to present not merely an effective criticism of traditional theory, but also a coherent, logically consistent, and complete theory as an alternative.

### 4. J. M. Keynes' 'general theory' of employment

Keynes' theory of income and employment determination, though surrounded with misunderstandings and obscurities at the time of publication, may be expressed today in a very simple and cogent way.

Once the basic process of income generation by effective demand has been stated (as in section 2 above), it is natural to go on to investigate what determines effective demand. Keynes, in a typically Classical manner, divides people into two broad categories: consumers and producers. Total effective demand is therefore the sum of demand for consumption goods ($C$) and demand for investment goods ($I$). And since effective demand generates income, we may simply write:

$$Y \equiv C + I. \tag{11.1}$$

One needs, at this point, a theory of consumption and a theory of investment.

Consumption is simply taken to depend on income. Keynes claims that on the whole and on the average, consumers tend to spend only a fraction – more precisely a decreasing fraction – of any increase in income. Therefore:

$$C = f(Y), \tag{11.2}$$

with the properties:

$$0 < f' < 1, \qquad f'' < 0,$$

where $f'$ represents the 'marginal propensity to consume', and its complement to unity, $(1 - f')$, the 'marginal propensity to save'. By using a simplified linear approximation, (11.2) may also be written as:

$$C = A + aY, \tag{11.2a}$$

where: $A =$ a positive constant, $a =$ marginal propensity to consume, (and $1 - a \equiv s$; marginal propensity to save).

As regards investment Keynes' theory is rather different.[18] Investments do not depend on income at all. In any given short-run situation (with a given technology and a given capital structure), the total amount of

---

[18] The contrast is immediately evident with traditional theory, where no analytical distinction is made between demand for consumption goods and demand for investment goods.

investment depends on the expected profitability of all possible investment projects and on the rate of interest. We may imagine entrepreneurs ranking all possible investment projects in order of decreasing profitability and then carrying out investments up to the point at which the expected rate of profit from the last project (called the 'marginal efficiency of capital') is just higher than, or equal to, the rate of interest, as expressing the cost of borrowing. (See fig. II.2.)

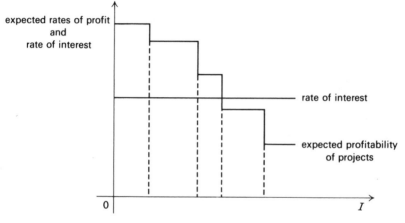

Fig. II.2

In synthesis we may write:

$$I = \varphi\,(E, i), \qquad (II.3)$$

where $E$ expresses the falling expected profitability of investments in the given conditions and $i$ is the rate of interest.

But at this point a new variable has been introduced – the rate of interest, which had been carefully kept out of the previous relations. Keynes is thereby induced, by the very logic of his system, to look for a new theory of the rate of interest. He claims that, for a series of reasons (transactions, precautionary, and speculative motives), there is a certain quantity of money that people are willing to hold at each level of the rate of interest. This quantity of money – the demand for money – is inversely related to the rate of interest, and tends to infinity before the rate of interest reaches zero (the liquidity preference schedule) Given this relation, the rate of interest will therefore be determined by the quantity of money $\bar{M}$ issued by the Central Authority – a purely monetary phenomenon. (See fig. II.3.)

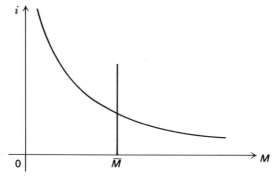

Fig. II.3

In synthesis we may write:

$$i = \psi(L, \bar{M}), \qquad (\text{II}.4)$$

where $L$ represents the falling liquidity preference schedule and $\bar{M}$ the quantity of money issued by the Central Authority.

To conclude, given the consumption function, the marginal efficiency of capital schedule and the liquidity preference schedule, and given the exogenously determined quantity $\bar{M}$, the four equations (II.1), (II.2), (II.3), (II.4), determine the four unknowns $Y, C, I, i.$[19]

The important novelty of this scheme, with respect to previous theories, is that it shows that there is no reason why the level of net national income should turn out to be precisely that level which entails the full utilization of productive capacity and the full employment of the labour force. When the system is left to itself, only by a fluke will full employment be achieved. The situation which Keynes regarded as normal is in fact one of less than full employment, as is shown in fig. II.4.

[19] Equations (II.3) and (II.4) are an elliptical, though effective, way of representing Keynes' determination of $I$ and $i$. A more detailed formalization would be to write each one of them as a set of two equations, the second of which represents an equilibrium relation, namely:

| | | | |
|---|---|---|---|
| $I = E(r)$, | (II.3a); | $M = L(i)$, | (II.4a) |
| $r = i$, | (II.3b); | $M = \bar{M}$, | (II.4b) |

where $r$ = expected rate of profit and $M$ = demand for money. In this case, we would say that the 6 equations (II.1), (II.2), (II.3a), (II.3b), (II.4a), (II.4b) determine the 6 unknowns: $Y, C, I, i, r, M$.

The important warning must, however, be added that these equations are only meant to represent a first approximation to Keynes' theory. Too much weight should not be laid upon them when considering situations which are far away from the equilibrium points. Moreover one should be careful when carrying out arguments which involve *shifts* of any curve. For the shifts of any one of these curves are not independent of the shifts of the others.

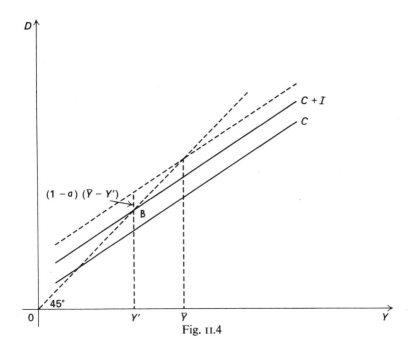

Fig. II.4

Demand for consumption is a function of income and demand for investment – determined independently of income – is simply added on to consumption. Equilibrium is attained at that point ($B$ in fig. II.4) where $C + I$ crosses the 45° line. At that point, total demand is equal to total production. Hence there *is* equilibrium between aggregate demand and aggregate supply. But it is an equilibrium of under-employment. And the difference ($\bar{Y} - Y'$) is there to represent idle capacity and unemployment.[20] This is the type of unemployment (due to lack of effective demand), which has become known by now as 'Keynesian' unemployment.

But the great practical relevance of this analysis is that not only does it give a neat diagnosis of one of the major weaknesses of the capitalist system. It also immediately suggests a powerful remedy. If (II.2) is substituted into (II.1), and $f(Y)$ is expanded in Taylor series (neglecting higher order terms) we obtain:

---

[20] In the whole of Keynesian analysis, idle capacity and unemployment are always used as synonymous, since, in the short run, they may be taken as proportional to each other.

$$Y(1 - f') = I, \tag{11.5}$$

and therefore:

$$\mathrm{d}Y = \frac{1}{1 - f'}\, \mathrm{d}I, \tag{11.6}$$

or, in the case of the linear consumption function (11.2a),

$$\mathrm{d}Y = \frac{1}{1 - a}\, \mathrm{d}I. \tag{11.7}$$

This is a remarkable relation. It says that any increase in the flow of new investment ($\mathrm{d}I$) will generate an increase in the flow of net income which is $\frac{1}{1 - f'}$ times as large ($\frac{1}{1 - a}$ times as large in the linear case). The expression $\frac{1}{1 - f'}$ (or $\frac{1}{1 - a}$) has therefore been called 'the multiplier'.[21] To give an idea of order of magnitude, if the marginal propensity to consume is 80 per cent, the multiplier is 5; meaning that any increase of investment will generate an increase of income five times as large. In the formulation considered here, where no relation contains any time lag, all effects are shown instantaneously ('instantaneous' multiplier)[22] and without any complication. Once this is understood, it becomes immediately evident that there is no necessity for the increase in effective demand to come from investment. *Any* autonomous increase in effective demand will generate precisely the same multiplicative effects. Therefore, when current investment is too low to bring about full employment, the Government can always step in with public expenditure (through deficit spending) and make a net addition to effective demand. Full employment may thereby be brought about by Government policy. As may be seen from fig. 11.4, given any function $C + I$, there always exists an amount of additional public

[21] It was discovered by Richard Kahn, in 'The Relation of Home Investment to Unemployment', *The Economic Journal*, 1931, pp. 173–98. It is, therefore, also referred to as the Kahn multiplier.

[22] The whole of Keynes' analysis is always carried out in these terms, i.e. as if the effects of the Kahn multiplier worked out instantaneously. It may, however, be useful, for certain purposes, to introduce a time lag between the reception of an income and the consumption of it. This gives rise to the 'lagged' multiplier, which is dealt with in an appendix to this essay.

expenditure – equal to $(1 - a)(\bar{Y} - Y')$ – which, if carried out, will take the system to the point of full employment.[23]

## 5. *The principle of effective demand in a different context*

It is important to distinguish, in Keynes' analysis, the principle of effective demand from the analytical tools he used in order to put it across. The basic enrichment that Keynes brought to economics is the principle of effective demand, but what gave Keynes' theory success were his analytical tools. Had he not developed them he would have failed (like all his predecessors) to convey the principle of effective demand. The distinction is important because all the discussions that centred around the *General Theory*, both at the time of publication and afterwards, have concentrated on Keynes' analytical tools; not on the principle of effective demand. Yet, by modifying Keynes' analytical tools, the critics have tried to slip behind Keynes' equations a quite different conception of economic behaviour, so as to minimize, or even render entirely irrelevant, the principle of effective demand.

In order to show that this principle is something quite distinct from Keynes' particular tools of analysis, it may be useful to re-state it in an entirely different context and independently of Keynes' theory. Consider an industrial economy as represented by what has become known as the Leontief closed system:[24]

$$\left\{ \begin{bmatrix} \mathbf{I} & \mathbf{0} \\ \mathbf{0}' & 1 \end{bmatrix} - \begin{bmatrix} \mathbf{A} & \mathbf{y} \\ \mathbf{a}_n & 0 \end{bmatrix} \right\} \begin{bmatrix} \mathbf{X} \\ N \end{bmatrix} = \begin{bmatrix} \mathbf{0} \\ 0 \end{bmatrix}, \tag{II.8}$$

where: $\mathbf{I}$ is a unit matrix of the same order as $\mathbf{A}$, the inter-industry commodity coefficient matrix; $\mathbf{a}_n$ is the (row) vector of labour-input coefficients, $\mathbf{y}$ is the (column) vector of per-capita final demand coefficients; $\mathbf{X}$ is the (column) vector of total production; $N$ is the available labour force; and $\mathbf{0}$ is the (column) zero vector. Expression (II.8) represents a linear and homogeneous system of equations. Therefore a necessary condition for non-trivial (i.e. non-zero) solutions is:

$$\det \left\{ \begin{bmatrix} \mathbf{I} & \mathbf{0} \\ \mathbf{0}' & 1 \end{bmatrix} - \begin{bmatrix} \mathbf{A} & \mathbf{y} \\ \mathbf{a}_n & 0 \end{bmatrix} \right\} = 0. \tag{II.9}$$

[23] The 'Keynesian' management of total effective demand has by now become such a common Government policy as to be used sometimes not only for achieving full employment, but also for deliberately *causing* 'Keynesian' unemployment.

[24] Wassily W. Leontief, *The Structure of American Economy, 1919–1929*, Cambridge Mass., 1941.

The determinant of the coefficient matrix must be equal to zero. Since $\mathbf{A}$ and $\mathbf{a}_n$ contain *technical* coefficients, which are given, the only coefficients which can adapt, if condition (11.9) is to be fulfilled, are the per-capita demand coefficients $\mathbf{y}$. This makes economic sense. Total demand for consumption and investment cannot be higher than, i.e. is limited by, the technological possibilities of the economic system. But (11.9) also means something more. Not only cannot the determinant of the coefficient matrix be higher than zero, it cannot be lower either, if the system of equations is to be satisfied. The economic meaning of this is straightforward. Total demand must be high enough as to require the full utilization of existing commodity stocks and the full employment of the existing labour force. If demand were too low, with respect to requirement (11.9), there would be idle productive capacity and unemployment of the labour force; if it were too high, there would be an inflationary situation. This is nothing but the principle of effective demand.

There is no reason, *a priori*, why condition (11.9) should always and automatically be satisfied. The trouble with pre-Keynesian economics was that it took for granted that (11.9) *is* always satisfied (Say's Law), and left the proof to the contrary to its opponents; who got muddled up. (Here Keynes had a quick answer: by breaking up total effective demand into two parts – consumption, as a fraction of income, and investment, independent of income – he could show that that equality can only be attained by a fluke.)

What misled pre-Keynesian economists is that, if (11.9) happens to be satisfied to begin with, then the total sum of personal incomes (wages and profits in Leontief's simple scheme) is exactly equal to full-employment net national income. They took this also to mean effective demand. But there is no reason to expect that the total sum of wages and profit should necessarily all be converted into effective demand (should all be spent) in the following period, which is the necessary condition for (11.9) to continue to be satisfied. There is no guarantee that full employment will be maintained, even if it happened to be realized to begin with.

## 6. *Ricardian features of Keynes' analysis*

We may now briefly consider Keynes' analytical tools. The most striking feature that emerges immediately is Keynes' clear break with the sixty-year-old tradition of marginal economic theory and his return to the methods of analysis of the earlier Classical economists of the beginning of the nineteenth century.

42

The whole conception of an economic system behind equations (11.1)–(11.4) is typically Classical. The use of macro-economic variables, the division of all economic agents into broad categories (consumers and entrepreneurs, in Keynes' case), the search for the determination of the rate of interest – and by implication of the distribution of income – in a sphere outside that of output – all these are features inherited from Classical economic analysis. Even the marginal-efficiency-of-capital schedule, which might, at a first superficial look, appear as belonging to marginal economic analysis, when examined more deeply turns out to have a rather different origin. Keynes' ranking of all investment projects in a decreasing order of profitability is more akin to Ricardo's ranking of all lands in a decreasing order of fertility than to any marginal economic elaboration. And in any case, there is absolutely no need to consider Keynes' marginal-efficiency-of-capital schedule as an expression of the marginal productivity theory of capital. This theory necessarily entails an inverse monotonic relation between capital intensity and the rate of interest. But that is not the case with Keynes' ranking of investment projects (fig. 11.3 above). In a slump situation the last project to be implemented might well be the least capital intensive of all, and therefore entail a decrease (not an increase) of the average amount of capital per employed labour.

Coming down to a more specific comparison, the analytical similarities that are most evident are with the Ricardian scheme. In spite of Keynes' own understandable enthusiasm for Malthus (in view of the latter's treatment of effective demand), and in spite of Keynes' frequent harsh remarks on Ricardo, it is basically the Ricardian method of analysis that Keynes has revived.[25] The most typical indication of this is to be found in the directness with which Keynes proceeds to state his assumptions. Like Ricardo, he is always looking for fundamentals. He singles out for consideration the variables he believes to be the most important. All the others, giving rise to unimportant complications – though, as he says, are always 'kept at the back of his head' for the

[25] Schumpeter perceived this very clearly when he wrote: 'the similarity between the aims and methods of those two eminent men, Keynes and Ricardo, is indeed striking, though it will not impress those who look primarily for the advice a writer tenders. Of course, there is a world between Keynes and Ricardo in this respect, and Keynes' views on economic policy bear much more resemblance to Malthus'. But I am speaking of Ricardo's and Keynes' methods of securing the clear-cut result. On this point they were brothers in the spirit.' (Joseph A. Schumpeter, *History of Economic Analysis*, New York, 1954, p. 473n.)

necessary qualifications[26] – are, for immediate purposes, frozen out by simple assumptions.

The characteristic consequence of this methodological procedure is the emergence in Keynes, as in Ricardo, of a system of equations of the 'causal type', or, as we may also say, of the 'decomposable type', as opposed to a completely interdependent system of simultaneous equations. If we go back to equations (II.1)–(II.4), we notice in them a very definite logical succession according to which the variables are determined (even if some of them may form among themselves smaller interdependent sub-systems). If we indicate the causal ordering[27] by an arrow, we may actually write:

$$\psi\,(L,\,\bar{M}) \to i \to \varphi(E,\,i) \to I \to \begin{cases} Y = C + I \\ C = f(Y) \end{cases} \begin{matrix} \nearrow Y, \\ \searrow C. \end{matrix}$$

In other words, function $\psi$ determines $i$ independently of anything else. Then, given $i$, function $\varphi$ determines $I$ independently of anything else; and finally, given $I$, equations (II.1) and (II.2) form among themselves a smaller interdependent sub-system, which simultaneously determines $Y$ and $C$.

As against the attitude – so common to marginal economics theorists – that 'everything depends on everything else', Keynes (as Ricardo) takes the opposite attitude that it is one of the tasks of the economic theorist himself also to specify which variables are sufficiently interdependent as to be best represented by simultaneous relations, and which variables exhibit such an overwhelming dependence in one direction (and such a small dependence in the opposite direction) as to be best represented by one-way-direction relations.[28]

---

[26] See Keynes' own description of this process, as contrasted with the 'symbolic pseudo-mathematical methods of formalising a system of economic analysis', on pp. 297–8 of the *General Theory*.

[27] Since the terms 'cause' and 'effect' have given rise to so many and so heated epistemological discussions, it may be useful to point out explicitly that there is no need to step onto controversial ground here. The term 'causal ordering' is here used simply in the sense of an asymmetrical relation among certain variables, namely as indicating a one-way direction in which, in a formal sense, the variables of the system are determined. This formal and non-controversial meaning of the term 'causal ordering' has been stressed and illustrated at length by Herbert Simon: 'Causal Ordering and Identifiability', in Wm. C. Hood and T. C. Koopmans (eds.) *Studies in Econometric Method*, New York, 1953, pp. 49–74.

[28] Schumpeter, whose ideal hero was neither Ricardo nor Keynes (but Walras) has found this method of analysis so contrary to his aesthetic sense of symmetry as to call it 'the Ricardian Vice'. (J. A. Schumpeter, *op. cit.* p. 473.) But there is no justification for such an abuse. Aesthetics is not necessarily the best criterion to use for economic analysis, and even less for economic policy.

The most remarkable example of the fruitfulness of this approach is given by that major piece of Keynes' analysis which has solved the problem of the relationship between investments and savings. On this point Keynes had challenged a well-established tenet of traditional theory, which maintained that savings and investments are simultaneously determined at that point where the rate of interest equates them. Keynes' alternative theory emerges from equations (II.1)–(II.4). $I$ is determined by (II.3) and (II.4), independently of anything else. Then equations (II.1) and (II.2) determine $Y$ and $C$. But since total savings $S$ are, by definition:

$$S \equiv Y - C, \qquad (\text{II}.10)$$

then it follows that:

$$S = I, \text{ in the sense that } I \to S. \qquad (\text{II}.11)$$

Total savings are, so to speak, an entirely passive variable, which always turns out to be equal to total investments, whatever the decisions to save may be. From Keynes' analysis, which is in terms of the instantaneous multiplier, this result follows immediately. But the same result is confirmed, and shown even better, by the use of the 'lagged' multiplier, which entails a long series of successive steps, during which decisions to save are seen to adapt themselves to investment, through changes in income. In the whole of this process – out of equilibrium as well as in equilibrium – actual savings are always, and at each step, equal to the predetermined amount of investments.[29]

The practical importance of these results has been decisive for the general acceptance of Keynes' theory. Whereas traditional economics, with all its complicated interdependences, had been unable to discriminate between what is important and what is unimportant, and had given recommendations which were at best inconclusive and sometimes downright wrong; Keynes was able to give clear, definite, and extremely powerful prescriptions of what to do in order to overcome slump situations.[30] This made him the most influential economist of our time.

### 7. *Anti-Keynesian features of some 'Keynesian' literature*

The economic literature that has followed the publication of the *General Theory* is by now immense. Some of it has no doubt contributed

---

[29] See the appendix to this essay.

[30] Thus, if we take conclusiveness as an alternative criterion to aesthetics, what Schumpeter calls 'the Ricardian Vice' might well be called a 'Ricardian Virtue'.

to clarifying obscurities and filling in gaps, before going over to dynamic analysis. But a great deal of it (and it has not been the least successful) has also been aimed at watering down Keynes' innovations – at attenuating the break with tradition and re-casting Keynes' analysis so as to 'digest' it into pre-Keynesian modes of thinking.[31]

It is not, of course, always easy in considering this 'Keynesian' literature, to pin-point exactly where Keynes' message gets distorted. But if the interpretation put forward in the previous pages is correct, then surely a most reliable sign of distortion shows up any time the original Keynes' 'clear-cut results' are obfuscated by the imposition of interdependences which transform Keynes' causally ordered relations into a system of simultaneous equations.

We may consider, as an illustrative example, the most popular of all textbook presentations of 'Keynesian' theory – the one given by Sir John Hicks.[32] Hicks is not, after all, an extreme anti-Keynesian. He immediately repudiates Pigou's theory of employment and accepts Keynes' method of stating major relations in aggregate terms. Yet his procedure is, I should say, typically un-Keynesian. After accepting equation (ii.1) above as an identity, he proceeds to give equation (ii.3) a marginal-productivity-of-capital interpretation. He then turns equation (ii.2) upside down by considering savings, instead of consumption, and – very significantly – he modifies it by introducing the rate of interest. Finally, he modifies equation (ii.4) by introducing income. In this way, consumption (but he says savings) is made to depend not only on income but also on the rate of interest, and demand for money is made to depend not only on the rate of interest but also on income. At the end of this, apparently innocuous, manipulation, Hicks has in fact broken up Keynes' basic chain of arguments. The relations have been turned into a system of simultaneous equations, i.e. precisely into what Keynes did *not* want them to be. Hicks exploits his procedure twice over by scolding Keynes for considering only what appears as a

---

[31] A critical attitude towards the various interpretations of Keynes has recently been stimulated by the works of Clower and Leijonhufvud (R. F. Clower, 'The Keynesian Counter-Revolution: a Theoretical Appraisal', in F. H. Hahn and F. Brechling (eds.), *The Theory of Interest Rates*, London, 1965, pp. 103–25; Axel Leijonhufvud, *On Keynesian Economics and the Economics of Keynes*, New York, 1968). Yet, while Clower's and Leijonhufvud's critical remarks have been salutary, their more positive suggestion, which amounts to a re-interpretation of Keynes' analysis within a Walrasian scheme, remains as questionable as all the others. For, we know that Keynes' immediate source in traditional economics was not Walras, whose works he knew very little, but Marshall.

[32] John R. Hicks, 'Mr Keynes and the "Classics"; a Suggested Interpretation', *Econometrica*, 1937, pp. 147–59.

'particular case' of his 'more general' model, namely the particular case in which the (surreptitiously) inserted variables have no influence.[33]

The device succeeds so well with reference to savings and investments as to make these regulated, in the traditional way, by the rate of interest, and to allow Hicks, if all were only to depend on that, even to bring back 'the Treasury view of 1929'![34] So Keynes' contribution on effective demand is wiped out at a stroke. The same device does not succeed so well with reference to the liquidity preference schedule, where inserting income does not bring back old monetary theory. Things however are left at that. Hicks contents himself with drawing his conclusion that the basic contribution of Keynes to economic analysis is simply represented by the liquidity-preference-theory of the rate of interest.[35]

But this is surely a distortion. However important a role liquidity preference may play in Keynes' monetary theory, it is entirely immaterial to his theory of effective demand. What this theory requires, as far as the rate of interest is concerned, is not that the rate of interest is determined by liquidity preference, but that it is determined *exogenously* with respect to the income generation process. Whether, in particular, liquidity preference, or anything else determines it, is entirely immaterial.

The Hicks reinterpretation also helps to illustrate how the replacement of causally ordered relations with a system of simultaneous equations is not used only as a purely formal device but as a medium to introduce a basically different interpretative model of economic reality. The process has been pushed much further by a host of subsequent writers. I should recall here that much of pre-Keynesian economic thought does not basically refer to an industrial society, but to a more primitive type of society, in which resources (taken as given) are being offered and at the same time represent the purchasing power of the single individuals. When pushed to the extreme, these concepts are shaped into a 'model of pure exchange', expressed precisely by a system of simultaneous equations (supply functions and demand functions), from which prices emerge as the solutions.

The re-casting of Keynes' analysis in terms of simultaneous equations is the necessary step to the resumption of such concepts. What inevitably happens is that, behind the formal *façade* of a simultaneous equation

[33] From a purely formal point of view, *any* relation can be said to be a 'particular case' of a 'more general' model in this way. It is enough to insert an extra variable, which 'generalizes' it, and then say that the previous relation is a 'particular case' of the new one.

[34] Hicks, *Econometrica*, 1937, p. 152n.

[35] The same conclusion is reiterated by Franco Modigliani, in 'Liquidity Preference and the Theory of Interest and Money', *Econometrica*, 1944, pp. 45–88.

system, a substitution of interpretative models takes place. The typical features of an industrial society are made to recede and the characteristic features of a rather imaginary 'exchange' economy are imperceptibly slipped in instead. Within such a context, it is not surprising that what is said by Keynes becomes more or less irrelevant, or can only appear as referring to 'imperfections' of the market, 'rigidities' of prices and wages, or 'liquidity traps'.

This is in fact the very basic distortion in so much of the 'Keynesian' literature: that what Keynes says with reference to an industrial society is reinterpreted as referring to something else – to a more primitive society, or sometimes even to a mythical society that never existed – where it can have either no meaning or no relevance. Unfortunately, the consequences are rather serious. The misleading impression is given that all problems of our time would disappear if only the 'rigidities' were to be eliminated. As if the 'rigidities' were the cause and not themselves one of the many inherent consequences of the industrial society in which we live.

## 8. *The principle of acceleration*

If a proof were needed at all of the independence of Keynes' theory of effective demand from the liquidity preference schedule, this proof is given by the development – independently of Keynes – of a theory of investment known as the principle of acceleration.[36] This theory is entirely based on effective demand and makes no reference whatever to the rate of interest.

The term 'principle of acceleration' (or simply 'accelerator') comes from the circumstance that an expected change in total demand tends to induce a larger change (an 'acceleration') of investments. If, for example, the capital stock were 400 and annual production were 100 (a capital–output ratio of 4), a change of 10 in annual production would tend to require an *addition* to the capital stock 4 times as large – i.e. an investment of 40. In general we may therefore write:

[36] Under different forms, the principle of acceleration has appeared long before the 1930s in the works of Aftalion, Bickerdike and J. M. Clark. (Albert Aftalion, 'La réalité des surproductions générales', *Revue d'Economie Politique*, 1909, pp. 219–20 and 'The Theory of Economic Cycles based on the Capitalistic Technique of Production', *The Review of Economic Statistics*, 1927. pp. 165–70; C. F. Bickerdike, 'A Non-Monetary Cause of Fluctuations in Employment', *The Economic Journal*, 1914, pp. 357–70; J. M. Clark, 'Business Acceleration and the Law of Demand: a Technical Factor in Economic Cycles', *The Journal of Political Economy*, 1917, pp. 217–35, and *Strategic Factors in Business Cycles*, New York, 1934.)

$$I = \Phi(\Delta Y^E), \tag{11.12}$$

i.e. investments as a function of the expected change in income ($\Delta Y^E$).

This expression, by itself, immediately suggests all the difficulties of giving the principle of acceleration a mathematical formulation. Expectations cannot be quantified or rather can only be quantified by using some proxy variables. In the 'accelerator' economic literature, the proxy variable for the expected change of income that is normally used is the *past* change of income. In other words, the assumption is made that entrepreneurs look at changes of national income in the past and take them as an indication of what to expect in the future (simple extrapolation). The simplest expression of the principle of acceleration has therefore become:

$$I_t = v(Y_{t-1} - Y_{t-2}), \tag{11.13}$$

where $v$ is a behavioural parameter. By calling $K =$ capital stock, this expression may also be written as:

$$I_t = v Y_{t-1} - K_{t-1}, \tag{11.14}$$

where[37] parameter $v$ may be interpreted as the *desired* capital–output ratio, and therefore $v Y_{t-1}$ as the desired stock of capital. Expression (11.14) says that entrepreneurs will carry out investments to cover the difference between the *desired* and the *actual* stock of capital.

This relation may be rendered a little more flexible by writing it as:

$$I_t = \beta (v Y_{t-1} - K_{t-1}), \qquad \text{where: } \beta \leq 1; \tag{11.15}$$

which reduces to (11.14) and (11.13) in the particular case in which $\beta = 1$. The idea is that, when there is a discrepancy between desired and actual capital–output ratio, entrepreneurs may not carry out investments to cover the full difference, but only a fraction of it. More neatly:

$$I_t = \alpha Y_{t-1} - \beta K_{t-1}, \qquad \text{where } \alpha = v\beta, \tag{11.16}$$

an expression also known as the 'capital stock adjustment principle'.[38]

From a purely formal point of view, the remarkable property of the principle of acceleration is that it provides a theory of investment

---

[37] By subtracting equation (11.14), from itself (but shifted by one period) we obtain:

$$I_t = v Y_{t-1} - K_{t-1},$$
$$I_{t-1} = v Y_{t-2} - K_{t-2},$$
$$\overline{I_t - I_{t-1} = v(Y_{t-1} - Y_{t-2}) - (K_{t-1} - K_{t-2}).}$$

This is nothing but equation (11.13) since $K_{t-1}, - K_{t-2} = I_{t-1}$.

[38] See, for example, R. C. O. Matthews, *The Trade Cycle*, Cambridge, 1959, pp. 40 ff.

symmetrical to the Keynesian theory of consumption (i.e. to the multiplier relation). Taken together, the multiplier and the accelerator give an explanation of both parts of total effective demand (consumption and investment) in terms of the same macro-economic variables. Keynes had explained why an economic system may fall into a depression. The principle of acceleration came also to explain how depressions can recur regularly. The introduction of *changes* in income immediately carried the investigation over to dynamic analysis. For, a change in income induces a larger change in investment (accelerator), and this change in investment generates an even larger change in income (multiplier). The analysis of this accelerator–multiplier interaction has given rise to practically all modern theories of the trade cycle.[39] These theories represent perhaps the culmination of the theory of effective demand.

## 9. *Final remarks*

The warning must be added that, in spite of the formal symmetry of the multiplier and the accelerator relations, there are substantial differences between the two. When income is inserted as the argument of the consumption function, that is precisely what is meant. But when a change of income is inserted as the argument of the investment function, that is not really what is meant. Ideally what should be inserted is the *expected* change in income. But since expectations cannot be quantified, we must be content with using the past change in income as a proxy variable for the expected change in income. This places the two equations at two quite different levels of abstraction, the one concerning the accelerator relation being the more remote of the two. The difficulty here is that one cannot hope to take this asymmetry into account by any mathematical formulation.[40] The theorist must therefore be keenly aware, in evaluating the conclusions, that at the point of departure there is an investment function that has a weaker theoretical foundation than the consumption function.

[39] The first to attribute explicitly the recurrence of depressions to the joint action of the multiplier and the accelerator seems to have been Roy Harrod in *The Trade Cycle – an Essay*, Oxford, 1936. See also E. Lundberg, *Studies in the Theory of Economic Expansion*, London, 1937.

[40] When equations (11.2a) and (11.16) are written side by side, and joint elaborations are carried out, these can make no distinction between the parameters coming from one relation and those coming from the other. All parameters are treated in the same way, though the assumptions behind them have a quite different reliability.

It may, moreover, be remarked that the multiplier relation always remains formally the same, whether the system is in a situation of idle productive capacity or in a situation of full capacity utilization (although in real terms the effects will of course be different). The principle of acceleration, on the other hand, works at its best in a situation of full capacity utilization. When there is idle capacity, the principle may still be working but in an attenuated form, or in any case in a more complicated way.[41]

All that this amounts to is that the results must be interpreted with care and judgment. If the analysis of the interaction of the multiplier and the accelerator has taken the economic theory of effective demand to its peak, it has also clearly strained it to the limits of its possibilities. For, as soon as economic investigation is carried over from the Keynesian short run to movements through time, and the capital stock can no longer be taken as given but is itself changing, then another side of the picture is bound to become relevant – the evolution through time of the physical possibilities of production.

## *APPENDIX*

### *The 'lagged' multiplier*

For completeness' sake, it may be useful to devote a few lines to the 'lagged' version, as opposed to the 'instantaneous' version, of the multiplier relation. The 'lagged' multiplier emerged mainly from the discussions of J. M. Keynes with Dennis Robertson and has the interesting property of showing in detail the process through which actual savings adapt to predetermined investments, through changes in income.

Let us consider what has been called a 'Robertsonian' consumption function, in which there is a time-lag between income and consumption:

$$C_t = A + aY_{t-1}, \tag{11.2b}$$

and let us take, in conjunction with it, relation:

$$Y_t \equiv C_t + I_t, \tag{11.1b}$$

to form a self-contained system in which $I_t$ is determined exogenously.

---

[41] One way of partially remedying this deficiency has been tried with the introduction of non-linearity. See especially: R. M. Goodwin, 'The Non-Linear Accelerator and the Persistence of Business Cycles', *Econometrica*, 1951, pp. 1–17.

Suppose now that investment, after being zero up to time $t = 0$, is then raised to a positive amount $I$ from $t = 1$ onwards. This means $I_t = 0$ and $Y_t = C_t$, for all $t = 0, -1, -2, \ldots$; but $I_t = I$ for all $t = 1, 2, 3, \ldots$. In successive periods, we have:

$$Y_0 = C_0 + I_0 = A + aY_{-1} = A + aY_0 = C_0,$$
$$S_0 = Y_0 - C_0 = 0,$$
$$Y_1 = C_1 + I = A + aY_0 + I = Y_0 + I,$$
$$S_1 = Y_1 - C_1 = I,$$
$$Y_2 = C_2 + I = A + aY_1 + I = A + a(Y_0 + I) + I = Y_0 + aI + I,$$
$$S_2 = Y_2 - C_2 = I,$$
$$Y_3 = C_3 + I = A + aY_2 + I = A + a(Y_0 + aI + I) + I = Y_0 + a^2 I + aI + I,$$
$$S_3 = Y_3 - C_3 = I,$$
$$\vdots$$
$$Y_n = C_n + I = A + aY_{n-1} + I = Y_0 + I(1 + a + a^2 + a^3 + \ldots a^{n-1}),$$
$$S_n = Y_n - C_n = I.$$

As may be seen, savings $S_t$ are always equal to the predetermined amount of investment $I$, at each single step, although income is increasing all the time (but at a decreasing rate, since $a < 1$).

If we call $\Delta Y = Y_n - Y_0$, the total increase of income from $t = 0$ to $t = n$, we obtain:

$$\Delta Y = Y_n - Y_0 = I(1 + a + a^2 + \ldots a^{n-1}),$$

or, using the formula for the sum of a geometric progression:

$$\Delta Y = I \frac{1 - a^{n-1}}{1 - a},$$

Since $a < 1$, $\Delta Y$ clearly tends to a finite limit as $n \to \infty$, i.e.

$$\lim_{n \to \infty} \Delta Y = \frac{1}{1 - a} I,$$

which precisely coincides with expression (II.7) obtained for the instantaneous multiplier. Thus when consumption decisions lag behind income, the total increase in income, given by the multiplier formula $1/(1 - a)$, will be obtained not immediately, but asymptotically, as time goes on. The process is illustrated in fig. II.5. At the beginning of the process towards the new equilibrium situation, there are big leaps – after only four or five steps, the system is already rather near the new equilibrium level of income $Y^*$. But since each step is smaller than the previous one, the process slows down as it goes on. The final position, though nearly approached after only the first few steps, is never quite reached exactly.

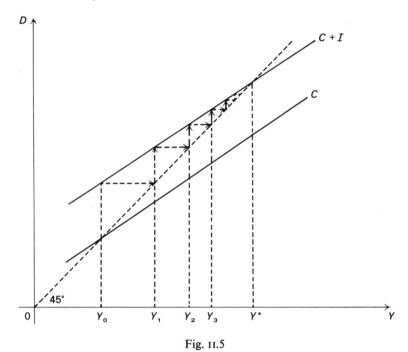

Fig. II.5

The interesting phenomenon to notice is that, during the whole process, the total savings that people intend to do, or *ex-ante* savings, $(Y_{t-1} - C_t)$, are different from the total savings they will in fact end up with doing, or *actual* savings, $(Y_t - C_t)$. *Ex-ante* savings, in fig. II.5, are the difference between the 45° line and function $C$, while *actual* savings are the difference between $(C + I)$ and $C$, and therefore always coincide with investment $I$.

To conclude, savings decisions are simply frustrated, as long as they differ from the predetermined amount of investment. Only when the system has actually reached the new equilibrium position, do *ex-ante* savings become equal to actual savings. In other words, savings decisions become effective only when the changes in income have made them yield an amount of savings equal to the predetermined amount of investment.

# III
# Cyclical fluctuations and economic growth*

The publication of J. M. Keynes' *General Theory* has been followed, especially in the Anglo-American economic literature, by a long series of macro-economic models, which have allowed their authors to present some simple explanations of two significant dynamic movements of an economic system as an aggregate: the cyclical fluctuations and the economic growth of the exponential type. The task of clarifying the relation between these two phenomena has turned out to be much more difficult. Economists have not so far been able to provide a theory which accounts for both of them and explains the economic movement of a capitalist society as it can be observed in the real world, where it conforms neither to pure cycles nor to a steady growth, but to a complex dynamic process of growth with periodic irregularities.

All models which have been presented may be classified in two groups. A first group – which began with the well-known Harrod–Domar model – aimed at defining a hypothetical path of steady growth, externally given by the *natural* possibilities of supply of the system, and then at finding the conditions of equilibrium which the economic magnitudes must satisfy in order to adhere to that movement. A second group has had a somewhat different aim. The attention has been focused, not on external data, but on some *endogenous* relations, expressing the aggregate behaviour of consumers (Keynesian multiplier) and of entrepreneurs (principle of acceleration), with the purpose of exploring the dynamic consequences of these two kinds of behaviour. By this type of analysis, various authors have come to different conclusions. Until not very long ago they at least agreed in saying that an economic system, if left to its purely endogenous forces, is not capable of steady growth but is inevitably doomed to periodic fluctuations (such fluctuations

* Originally published in Italian as 'Fluttuazioni cicliche e sviluppo economico', *l'industria*, no. 1, 1960, pp. 18–50; and then in English in *Oxford Economic Papers*, new series, vol. 12, no. 2, June 1960, pp. 215–41.

being then interpreted in different ways).[1] Recently, however, Professor Duesenberry[2] has presented a purely endogenous model which nevertheless produces a steady growth.

The time has come to enquire more deeply into this problem, which is what I propose to do in part I of the present essay, where the properties of an endogenous dynamic model, more general than those so far analysed in post-Keynesian literature, will be examined, with the help of a mathematical appendix. The model will enable us to explore not only the different dynamic movements which may follow from the interaction between the multiplier and the principle of acceleration, but also the consequences on the stability of the system deriving from the interrelations between the movements of income and those of the stock of capital.

A theoretical framework of this type will then make it possible to present, in part II of the essay, the various macro-economic theories so far proposed as particular cases of it.

This will allow us to single out the reasons why all these theories, though able to give separate explanations of a cyclical movement or of a growth movement, are unable to explain both phenomena together. Such reasons, which will turn out to be deeply connected with the macro-economic character of these models, will lead in the last section of the essay to outline a type of analysis of a more disaggregated nature, which – I hope – may help to shed new light on the whole complex and intricate problem of the relation existing between economic growth and cyclical fluctuations.

I

## 1. *The model*

Let us begin by an investigation of the dynamic behaviour of total effective demand in an economic system. We shall use for the purpose the following theoretical model:

[1] See, for example, R. Frisch, 'Propagation Problems and Impulse Problems in Dynamic Economics', in *Economic Essays in Honour of Gustav Cassel*, London, 1933, pp. 171–205; M. Kalecki, 'A Macro-dynamic Theory of Business Cycles', *Econometrica*, 1935, pp. 327–44; N. Kaldor, 'A Model of the Trade Cycle', *Economic Journal*, 1940, pp. 78–92; V. Marrama, 'Short Notes on a Model of the Trade Cycle', *The Review of Economic Studies*, 1946–7, pp. 34–40; J. R. Hicks, *A Contribution to the Theory of the Trade Cycle*, Oxford, 1950; R. M. Goodwin, 'The Non-Linear Accelerator and the Persistence of Business Cycles', *Econometrica*, 1951, pp. 1–17.

[2] J. S. Duesenberry, *Business Cycles and Economic Growth*, New York, 1958.

$$K_t \equiv K_{t-1} + I_t, \qquad \text{(III.1)}$$

$$Y_t \equiv C_t + I_t, \qquad \text{(III.2)}$$

$$C_t = aY_{t-1}, \qquad \text{(III.3)}$$

$$I_t = \alpha Y_{t-1} - \beta K_{t-1}, \qquad \text{(III.4)}$$

where: $I$ = total net investment, $C$ = total consumption, $Y$ = total effective demand, or total net income, $K$ = stock of capital at the end of the period under consideration, $t$ = period of time which the variables refer to. The variable $K$ represents a *stock* at the end of period $t$; all other variables express *flows* which take place during period $t$.

The system (III.1)–(III.4) is made up of four equations in four variables and is of a purely *endogenous* character. Equations (III.1) and (III.2) are identities; (III.3) represents total consumption as a simple linear function of income, where $0 < a < 1$; and (III.4) expresses total net investment as a linear positive function of income and a negative function of the stock of capital (so that $\alpha > 0$, $\beta > 0$).

Following a convention which is common to all cycle models, all variables will be interpreted in terms of *deviations* (positive or negative) from their values corresponding to the *stationary state*, intending by stationary state that situation where there is no net investment and total net income is equal to total consumption. In graphical terms, this situation corresponds to the point where the Keynesian consumption function intersects the 45° line through the origin. This, by the way, explains why (III.3) has been written in homogeneous terms (namely, without the constant term which normally appears in a Keynesian consumption function).

## 2. A graphical device

Model (III.1)–(III.4) is more general than those of Samuelson and of Hicks[3] because the investment function has been based on a more general form of the acceleration principle. In fact, we may write equation (III.4) as follows:[4]

$$I_t = \beta \left( \frac{\alpha}{\beta} Y_{t-1} - K_{t-1} \right), \qquad \text{(III.4a)}$$

[3] P. A. Samuelson, 'Interactions between the Multiplier Analysis and the Principle of Acceleration', *The Review of Economic Statistics*, 1939, pp. 75–8; Hicks, *A Contribution to the Theory of the Trade Cycle*.

[4] In the particular case in which $\beta = 1$, equation (III.4a) reduces to the simple acceleration principle adopted by Samuelson and Hicks.

where $\alpha/\beta$ may be interpreted as the ratio that entrepreneurs desire to keep between the capital stock and production per unit of time, and $\beta$ as the reciprocal of the number of periods over which entrepreneurs tend to distribute their investment whenever they find that the quantity of existing capital differs from the quantity which they desire to have.[5]

The model coincides, instead, with the one which has been adopted by Duesenberry in his latest book,[6] except for a few unimportant modifications. Duesenberry uses a device which is worth considering immediately. In terms of our model, he substitutes (III.1)–(III.2) into (III.3)–(III.4) and writes:

$$\frac{Y_t - Y_{t-1}}{Y_{t-1}} = (\alpha + a - 1) - \beta\,\frac{K_{t-1}}{Y_{t-1}}, \qquad \text{(III.5)}$$

$$\frac{K_t - K_{t-1}}{K_{t-1}} = -\beta + \alpha\,\frac{Y_{t-1}}{K_{t-1}}. \qquad \text{(III.6)}$$

By now calling: $r_y = \dfrac{Y_t - Y_{t-1}}{Y_{t-1}}$; $\quad r_k = \dfrac{K_t - K_{t-1}}{K_{t-1}}$; $\quad v = \dfrac{K_{t-1}}{Y_{t-1}}$,

(III.5)–(III.6) become:

$$r_y = (\alpha + a - 1) - \beta v, \qquad \text{(III.7)}$$

$$r_k = -\beta + \alpha\,\frac{1}{v}, \qquad \text{(III.8)}$$

which express the proportional rates of growth of income and capital ($r_y$ and $r_k$) as linear functions of the capital–output ratio ($v$), or of its reciprocal. These two equations can be represented graphically on a single diagram with the rates of growth on the ordinate and the capital–output ratio on the abscissa. The first equation is a straight line intercepting the ordinate at $(\alpha + a - 1)$ with a negative slope $-\beta$. The other equation is a rectangular hyperbola. Duesenberry always represents it[7] *as if* its asymptotes were the abscissa and the ordinate, but his diagrams are not correct. Equation (III.8) is indeed a rectangular hyperbola but only one of its asymptotes coincides with an axis (the ordinate). The other asymptote is a straight line parallel to the abscissa and displaced downwards by a distance $\beta$ (see fig. III.1). The diagram

---

[5] On this subject: R. M. Goodwin, 'Secular and Cyclical Aspects of the Multiplier and the Accelerator', in *Income Employment and Public Policy: Essays in Honor of A. H. Hansen*, New York, 1948, pp. 108–32; H. B. Chenery, 'Overcapacity and the Acceleration Principle', *Econometrica*, 1952, pp. 1–28.

[6] Duesenberry, *op. cit.*

[7] Duesenberry, *op. cit.*, pp. 205, 211, 220.

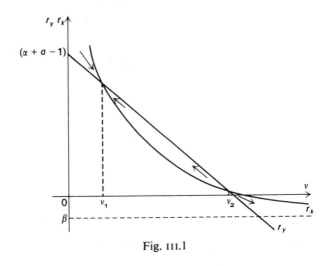

Fig. III.1

immediately suggests that curves (III.7)–(III.8) may not cross each other, or, if they do, they present two points of intersection (except in the limiting case when they are tangential and have therefore a single point in common). Therefore, in the case in which they cross each other, there are two values of the capital–output ratio – indicated by $v_1$ and $v_2$ in fig. III.1 – at which the proportional rate of growth of income is equal to the proportional rate of growth of capital. It appears from fig. III.1 that the rates of growth of income and of capital will change from one period to the next, unless the system is exactly in one of the two positions where the capital–output ratio is either $v_1$ or $v_2$. Of these two positions, however, only the first one fulfils the conditions for a stable dynamic equilibrium; position $v_2$ is unstable, in the sense that even if we suppose that the system may get there by chance, it will again diverge from there as soon as it is slightly displaced.

With a theoretical apparatus of this type, Duesenberry is able to affirm, contrary to all previous economists who elaborated endogenous theories of fluctuations, that an economic system which is governed by the multiplier–accelerator mechanism is capable of growing steadily. There are, however, two cases in which steady growth may be prevented: (i) when the parameters are such that the two curves (III.7)–(III.8) do not cross each other, and (ii) when, although the two curves cross each other, the system starts from a position in which the capital–output ratio is higher than $v_2$. Duesenberry excludes the first case from his analysis and focuses his attention exclusively on the second. He then tries to explain all the depressions of the United States economy in the last 100 years by looking for causes which are specific to each of them, and which have produced such shocks as to displace the system beyond its limits of stability.

But the model under consideration is more general than appears from Duesenberry's diagrams. The case in which the two curves do not intersect – which Duesenberry does consider, as pointed out above, but dismisses too quickly[8] – precisely corresponds to the situation on which the whole previous economic literature has relied in order to explain the regularities of business cycles. To demonstrate this proposition, we must abandon Duesenberry's analytical tools, which are no longer sufficient for the purpose, and turn to an explicit solution of the difference equations resulting from the model we are considering.

### 3. *The dynamics of income*

Let us go back to the system of equations (III.1)–(III.4) and let us substitute (III.1)–(III.2) into (III.3)–(III.4). We obtain:

$$K_t - K_{t-1} = \alpha Y_{t-1} - \beta K_{t-1}, \tag{III.9}$$

$$Y_t = (\alpha + a) Y_{t-1} - \beta K_{t-1}. \tag{III.10}$$

An expression for $K$ immediately emerges from (III.10), i.e.

$$K_{t-1} = \frac{\alpha + a}{\beta} Y_{t-1} - \frac{1}{\beta} Y_t. \tag{III.11}$$

By subtracting (III.9) from (III.10) and simplifying, we have:

$$Y_t - K_t + K_{t-1} = a Y_{t-1},$$

where the $K$'s may now be expressed in terms of the variable $Y$, by using (III.11). Substituting and simplifying, we finally obtain:

$$Y_t = (\alpha + a + 1 - \beta) Y_{t-1} - (\alpha + a - a\beta) Y_{t-2}. \tag{III.12}$$

This expression contains the parameters of both the consumption function and the investment function, and therefore expresses the joint effect of these two relations (multiplier–accelerator mechanism) on the dynamics of income. It belongs to a family of equations that

---

[8] He simply expresses the view that this case is unlikely to happen. He explains it shortly by saying that 'given appropriate initial conditions, income may grow at first' but will eventually stop rising and cause a depression, during which there is capital decumulation. He concludes that 'there appears to be no example of that type of depression'. Duesenberry, *op. cit.*, pp. 236 and 332.

mathematicians call homogeneous, second-order difference equations, and its general solution takes the following form:[9]

$$Y_t = A_1 x_1{}^t + A_2 x_2{}^t, \qquad (\text{III}.13)$$

where $A_1$ and $A_2$ are two arbitrary constants and $x_1$, $x_2$ are the roots of the quadratic equation:

$$x^2 - (\alpha + a + 1 - \beta)x + (\alpha + a - a\beta) = 0, \qquad (\text{III}.14)$$

namely:

$$x_{1,2} = \tfrac{1}{2}(\alpha + a + 1 - \beta) \pm \tfrac{1}{2}\sqrt{\{(\alpha + a + 1 - \beta)^2 - 4(\alpha + a - a\beta)\}}. \qquad (\text{III}.15)$$

Evidently, as $t$ increases in (III.13), the movement of $Y$ over time depends on the constants $A_1$, $A_2$ and on the nature of the roots $x_1$, $x_2$. Leaving to section 5 an examination of the meaning of the constants, and supposing here that they are positive, let us concentrate on the roots $x_1$, $x_2$.

From (III.15) it appears that $x_1$ and $x_2$ may be either real numbers or complex numbers, according as to whether the term under the square root is positive or negative, which depends on the values of the parameters $\alpha$, $\beta$, $a$. If $x_1$ and $x_2$ are real numbers, the behaviour of $Y$, after a few periods, will practically be dominated by that term in (III.13) which contains the larger of $x_1$, $x_2$ in absolute value. If $x_1$ and $x_2$ come out as complex numbers, (III.13) becomes more difficult to interpret. However, it can be transformed (see the mathematical appendix) in such a way as to obtain an expression, containing only *real* terms, of the following form:

$$Y_t = B\rho^t \cos(t\theta + \varepsilon), \qquad (\text{III}.16)$$

where the cos term represents the trigonometric function cosine; $B$, $\varepsilon$ are two arbitrary constants, and $\rho$, $\theta$ are two coefficients deriving from a particular combination of the parameters of equations (III.3)–(III.4).

Expressions (III.13) and (III.16), in their general formulation, are not enough, however, to provide a complete picture of all the possible dynamic movements of $Y$, because such movements may be of very different natures according to the values taken by the parameters which enter into the expressions. To find out the properties of all these possible movements, a long and patient examination is required, which has been developed in a mathematical appendix at the end of the essay.

[9] See, for example, W. J. Baumol, *Economic Dynamics*, New York, 1951; R. G. D. Allen, *Mathematical Economics*, London, 1956, ch. 6.

The conclusions, however, will be given here.

First of all, in order that there may exist any possibility of growth at all, a necessary condition is:

$$\alpha > 1 - a, \qquad (\text{III}.17)$$

which means that – for any given amount of capital – the marginal propensity to invest, as income increases, must be higher than the marginal propensity to save. If $\alpha$ were smaller than $(1 - a)$, the system would never be able to depart permanently from a situation of zero savings. In terms of fig. III.1, (III.17) means that the straight line must cut the ordinate in the positive range. Furthermore, another condition has to be imposed in order to rule out the possibility of some very peculiar behaviour of the system, contrary to any past or foreseeable experience. The condition is:

$$\beta < \alpha + a + 1, \qquad (\text{III}.18)$$

and is practically always satisfied, as can be realized by remembering the meaning of $\beta$ given at the beginning of section 2, and considering that $a$ is slightly less than one. In fact, condition (III.18) comes roughly to saying that the time-lag with which capital (by new investment) tends to be adapted to changes in income must not be less than a half of the time-lag (which is of one period) with which *consumption* is adapted to the same variation of income – a condition the non-fulfilment of which is very hard to conceive.

TABLE III.1

| Case no. | Range of values for $\beta$ | Type of roots | Time paths of Y and K (on the assumption $A_1 > 0$) |
|---|---|---|---|
| 1 | $0 \leqslant \beta \leqslant (\alpha + 1 - a) - 2\sqrt{\{\alpha(1-a)\}}$ | Real, positive, greater than one | Exponential positive growth |
| 2 | $(\alpha + 1 - a) - 2\sqrt{\{\alpha(1-a)\}} < \beta < \dfrac{\alpha + a - 1}{a}$ | Complex, with modulus ($\rho$) greater than one | Regular cycles of continuously increasing amplitude (*explosive*) |
| 3 | $\dfrac{\alpha + a - 1}{a} < \beta < (\alpha + 1 - a) + 2\sqrt{\{\alpha(1-a)\}}$ | Complex, with modulus ($\rho$) smaller than one | Regular cycles of continuously decreasing amplitude finally dying out at zero (*damped*) |
| 4 | $(\alpha + 1 - a) + 2\sqrt{\{\alpha(1-a)\}} \leqslant \beta < (\alpha + a + 1)$ | Real, positive, or one positive and one negative, smaller than one in absolute terms | Steady convergency towards zero (i.e. negative rate of growth) |

When (III.17) and (III.18) are satisfied, the movement of income over time may be of any of four different types which can be classified according to the range of values in which the parameter $\beta$ falls, relatively to the other parameters. The properties of these four types of behaviour are summarized in table III.1, and are separately illustrated by fig. III.2 to which the reader is now referred.

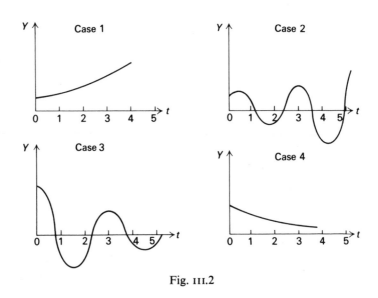

Fig. III.2

An interesting sub-case may be added to the four cases shown, as a limiting possibility between cases 2 and 3, when $\beta$ is exactly equal to $(\alpha + a - 1)/a$, and fluctuations maintain therefore not only a constant length but also a constant amplitude as time goes on.

The different types of dynamic behaviour which are described in table III.1 and illustrated in fig. III.2 synthesize in themselves the essential characteristics of all relevant cases which the endogenous mechanism of the multiplier–accelerator may call into being.[10] We shall now have to examine the interpretative value of these types of behaviour, but, before doing that, we must widen our analysis to enquire also into the possible dynamic movements of the stock of capital.

[10] The reader who is acquainted with the literature on the trade cycle will notice the similarity of the results which appear in the fourth column of table III.1 with those which emerge from the studies by Samuelson, *The Review of Economic Statistics*, 1939, and Hicks, *A Contribution to the Theory of the Trade Cycle*, on the interaction between the multiplier and the acceleration principle.

## 4. *The dynamics of the stock of capital*

As a consequence of the dynamic movement of that part of effective demand which refers to investment, the quantity of capital also changes in time, as income changes. In the foregoing section we have already obtained, for capital, equation (III.11), which expresses $K$ in terms of $Y$, namely in terms of the variable of which we have studied the dynamic behaviour. By now substituting (III.13) and (III.16) successively into (III.11), the following two expressions emerge:

$$K_t = v_1 A_1 x_1{}^t + v_2 A_2 x_2{}^t, \tag{III.19}$$

$$K_t = B\gamma\rho^t\cos(t\theta + \varepsilon - \eta), \tag{III.20}$$

which allow us to analyse the dynamic movement of $K$ in the case in which $x_1$ and $x_2$ are real and in the case in which they are complex numbers, respectively.

As can be seen immediately, (III.19) and (III.20) are similar to (III.13) and (III.16), the only difference being that they contain some more constants: $v_1$, $v_2$, $\gamma$, $\eta$. The possible movements of $K$ over time are therefore of the same type as those of $Y$, corresponding to the same ranges of values for $\beta$. They only differ by some fixed proportions (owing to constants $v_1$, $v_2$ in (III.19), and $\gamma$ in (III.20), all of which are shown to be positive in the appendix), and moreover by the constant $\eta$ in (III.20), which causes the fluctuations of capital to have a time-lag of a fraction of a period $(\eta/\theta)$ relative to the fluctuations of income.

## 5. *Interrelations between the dynamics of income and the dynamics of capital*

Our analysis has been carried on so far without enquiring into the meaning of those magnitudes which we have called 'arbitrary constants' – $A_1$, $A_2$, in the case of real solutions and $B$, $\varepsilon$, in the case of complex solutions. We have simply assumed that these constants are positive. In the case of complex roots such an assumption has no relevance because the signs of $B$ and $\varepsilon$, whatever they may be, do not modify qualitatively the dynamic behaviour of $Y$ and $K$ already described, as can be seen at once by inspecting (III.16) and (III.20). But in the case of real solutions the problem becomes more complicated and needs a deeper examination. This will also allow us to give a more rigorous meaning to the cumulative processes which already could be inferred from the graphical representation of fig. III.1.

The constants $A_1$ and $A_2$ have been called 'arbitrary' because they may be chosen arbitrarily in the solution of (III.11) and (III.12). This enables us to introduce in our problem two more *data*, and we may choose total income and total capital at period zero ($Y_0$ and $K_0$ – initial conditions of the system). By now putting $t = 0$ in (III.13) and (III.19) and solving for $A_1$ and $A_2$, we obtain (see the mathematical appendix for details):

$$A_1 = (v_2 Y_0 - K_0)/(v_2 - v_1), \qquad \text{(III.21)}$$

$$A_2 = (K_0 - v_1 Y_0)/(v_2 - v_1), \qquad \text{(III.22)}$$

where $A_1$ and $A_2$ are expressed in terms of the initial conditions ($Y_0$, $K_0$) and of the constants $v_1$, $v_2$. The last two constants come from a well-defined combination of the parameters of the system and it is shown in the appendix that they are both positive and that they correspond exactly to the $v_1$ and $v_2$ of fig. III.1. Moreover, $v_2$ is always greater than $v_1$. Now, of the two constants $A_1$ and $A_2$, only that one which is associated with the higher root among the $x_1$, $x_2$ becomes relevant because, as $t$ increases, the term containing the higher $x$ in (III.13) and (III.19) will become greater and greater with respect to the term containing the lower $x$ and will dominate it after a few periods. Since the higher root in absolute value, within the limits in which we are interested, is always $x_1$, then $A_1$ becomes the single constant which is relevant and which we must examine in detail.

Now (III.21) shows that, as $v_2 > v_1$, $A_1$ is positive or negative according as $K_0/Y_0$ (the ratio of initial capital to initial income) is smaller or greater than $v_2$. This gives paramount importance to the initial conditions and to the constant $v_2$, which comes in this way to represent an important critical value of the capital–output ratio. A radically different behaviour of the system corresponds to the two cases in which $A_1$ is positive – $(K_0/Y_0) < v_2$ – or negative – $(K_0/Y_0) > v_2$. If the system starts with a capital–output ratio smaller than $v_2$, income and capital move through time in the normal way described in the previous section. But if, as an initial condition or as a result of any external 'shock', the capital–output ratio turns out to be greater than $v_2$, the constant $A_1$ becomes negative and the dynamic paths of $Y$ and $K$, as $t$ increases, emerge as very different from those shown in the last column of Table III.1. More precisely, a negative $A_1$ – as appears from (III.13) and (III.19) – causes a negative cumulative movement in case 1 and a movement of convergency towards zero, but from the negative side, in case 4. Our analysis, however, can help us very little in these cases because it has been developed in order to determine what will happen *eventually* (as $t$ increases), while the system will never allow its endogenous forces to operate freely after a few periods. Indeed, after a while during which income and capital are decreasing, some external elements – such as limits to contraction of consumption, to decumulation of capital, etc. – will soon check the endogenous dynamism of the system, and the interpretative value of our equations breaks down. The only thing the model can tell us, therefore, when $(K_0/Y_0) > v_2$, is that the system is driven towards a slump. Without being able to indicate what will happen then, the model shows, moreover, that capital and income will not resume growth until their proportion is reduced below $v_2$.

By looking finally at the relative behaviour of income and capital in time, an interesting meaning also emerges for the other constant, $v_1$. Once more I must refer the reader to the mathematical appendix for a rigorous demonstration, but the result can be stated simply by saying that, in the case in which the system is capable of growing, income and capital tend asymptotically to a very definite proportion as time goes on, which exactly corresponds to $v_1$. The result is valid wherever the system starts from (excluding, of course, from the interpretation, values of $K_0/Y_0$ greater than $v_2$) and proves that the growing system is stable within a certain range. In other words, it shows that, when the conditions for an endogenous steady growth are satisfied, the system is capable of absorbing external 'shocks' in the sense that it tends to reproduce its equilibrium proportions whenever it is displaced from them, provided that the displacement does not upset the system beyond a certain critical value, which is represented in our case by a ratio of capital to income equal to $v_2$.

At this point I shall stop the analytical inquiry into the properties of the system of equations stated at the beginning. The results so far obtained are more than sufficient for the purposes of the present essay.

II

6. *The various interpretations of the endogenous dynamics of an economic system*

The investigation which has been patiently carried out in the appendix and summarized in the foregoing sections has by now placed us in a convenient position for putting into a single framework the various macro-dynamic theories of business cycles which have appeared during the last thirty years.

All these theories have the common feature of being based on an endogenous dynamism resulting from the interaction between the multiplier and some form of acceleration principle. The latter may be framed in a number of ways, but the results are always the same. According to the range of values in which the parameters of the investment function fall, the system produces four main types of behaviour: exponential growth, explosive cycles, damped cycles, steady contraction; to which the possibility of constant cycles may be added as a limiting case between the second and the third types of behaviour. The case of steady contraction has been unanimously dismissed as contrary to common experience; different authors have then reached different conclusions simply by taking up in turn one of the other possible outcomes of the same theoretical model.

The early theories (Frisch, Kalecki[11]) relied on that range of parameters which produces damped fluctuations. In order then, to explain the persistence of cycles, a theory was added about external and erratic 'shocks', which come continuously to stir up a cyclical movement which otherwise would slowly die out. The choice of the values of the parameters was based on the commonsense proposition that a system cannot get permanently away from its equilibrium position. What passed unnoticed, however, was the arbitrary association of the *equilibrium* position with the stationary state.

A similar line of thought characterizes a second type of theories (Kaldor, Marrama, Goodwin), which concentrated on regular fluctuations of neither explosive nor damped type. In order to avoid reliance on fortuitous coincidences, the persistence of cycles was explained in this case with the help of non-linear functions changing the behaviour of investments (in a continuous or discontinuous way) as the system goes farther and farther away from its equilibrium position.

Professor Hicks went a step further. While keeping the assumptions of linearity, he focused his attention on the case of explosive fluctuations, presenting them as 'constrained' by a 'floor', set by physical limits to contraction (gross investments cannot become negative), and by a 'ceiling', determined by the *natural* possibilities of the system to grow; a concept which meanwhile had made its appearance in economic analysis.[12] In this case too, the disregard of the growth range was based more on the emotional appeal of the impossibility of an 'explosive' system than on convincing arguments. But the terminology itself comes to be misleading in this context because a growing system is indeed

---

[11] The works which are referred to here and in the following sections are those which have been already mentioned.

[12] The concept was coined by Roy Harrod, *Towards a Dynamic Economics*, London, 1948.

'exploding', i.e. moving away, if we take the stationary state as a term of reference. The problem, of course, does not lie in the 'explosion' as such, but in whether it takes place at a reasonable rate, namely at a rate that can be coped with by the natural increase of population and of technical knowledge.

Finally, Duesenberry has lately concentrated on that range of the parameters which produces endogenous and steady growth. In this case, exclusion of regular fluctuations has come about in a more complicated and not at all clear way. It must be said, however, that Duesenberry has introduced something new in this type of analysis, namely the simultaneous treatment of the dynamics of capital, side by side with the dynamics of income. This has drawn attention to the relevance of the initial conditions from which the system may start after any external shock.

At this point the range of possibilities offered by the endogenous mechanism of the multiplier–accelerator seems to have been exhausted. Indeed, it is interesting to look, *ex-post*, at all this theoretical development. But it is also surprising to realize that, although the various authors have implicitly shown well-defined preferences for some particular values of the parameters of the investment function, they have not developed any explicit discussion to justify their positions.

## 7. *Possibility of a steady growth*

An interesting discussion – the only one to my knowledge – on the probability that the behavioural parameters of an economic system may fall in one or the other of the various mentioned intervals has been developed by Sidney Alexander,[13] and it seems to have been rather neglected by trade-cycle economists. Alexander starts from Samuelson's previous study[14] and, after a long analysis, comes to the conclusion that the behavioural parameters which produce a steady growth are possible but not very probable, because they would entail rather high rates of growth of the system, unless the propensity to consume is close to unity. His analysis, however, is carried out in terms of an investment function based on the simplest version of the acceleration principle (see our discussion at the beginning of section 2), and, although the author then drops the rigid hypotheses he starts from, he always remains linked to that frame of reference. Most of all, he is impressed very much by the value of the capital–output ratio which may be

[13] S. S. Alexander, 'The Accelerator as a Generator of Steady Growth', *The Quarterly Journal of Economics*, 1949, pp. 174–97.

[14] Samuelson, *The Review of Economic Statistics*, 1939.

observed in an economic system as a whole. Now, there is no reason to suppose that an investment function which represents the behaviour of entrepreneurs in response to *variations* of income should necessarily be based on proportions which are observed in the average of the system.

Our analysis, which has been developed with a more general and flexible version of the acceleration principle, puts us in a better position to evaluate the problem. A short discussion has been carried out on the subject in section 13 of the mathematical appendix. It is there shown that, for any predetermined value of the propensity to consume and for any predetermined rate of growth of the system, there always exists a couple of non-negative values of the two parameters of the investment function; in other words, there always exist an $\alpha$ (expressing the marginal response of entrepreneurs to a variation of income) and a $1/\beta$ (i.e. a number of periods for the tendency to spread investment over time) such as to lead the system to a path of exponential growth at a rate of change which is equal to the predetermined one. That is to say, at least as far as the dynamic movement of *effective* demand is concerned, there is no path of exponential growth, at a large or small rate of change as we may choose, that cannot be reached, provided that entrepreneurs adapt their behaviour (i.e. parameters $\alpha$ and $\beta$) to it.

From a formal point of view, the theorists of economic growth who have elaborated macro-dynamic models belonging to the first group mentioned in the introductory note, have followed a procedure which is very similar to the way of reasoning just hinted at. Taking as a reference the Harrod model – which has been the starting-point for all the others – we can see that the procedure has been to define first a path of growth made possible by external elements (population increase and technical progress), and then to find out the conditions that the behavioural functions of the system must satisfy in order that the path of growth externally defined may be adhered to. That does not imply that the externally defined path of growth should necessarily be reached as an effect of the endogenous forces. The problem is really left open. Indeed, the theoretical construction we have analysed does not contain any mechanism for the parameters expressing the behaviour of the system to fall in the exponential growth interval or in any one of the other intervals.

We may draw the conclusion, therefore, that no reason emerges, simply from an examination of the multiplier–accelerator dynamic process, for preferring the one or the other of the proposed interpretations of the economic dynamics based on it. The question is not even likely to be settled by empirical tests. Not only are there many practical difficulties in associating real movements to one or to the other type of behaviour; but moreover it will never be possible to observe a whole economic fluctuation as it would come out from the purely endogenous behaviour of the system, because any Government by now – progressive or conservative as it may be – is inevitably bound to make some sort of intervention any time it is faced with a movement into depression.

## 8. *The difficulties of providing a theory which may explain both cycles and growth*

The state of indeterminateness of the theoretical construction, which has emerged at the end of the foregoing section, contains in itself, as a particular consequence, the difficulties already hinted at of presenting a theory which may explain both fluctuations and growth. The situation is that, on the one hand, the macro-economic models which provide a cyclical interpretation of the economic activity cannot give any explanation of economic growth, and, on the other hand, those theories which define, or rely on, the conditions for a dynamic equilibrium to be reached and maintained cannot give an explanation of business cycles.[15]

From a theoretical point of view, the situation would not be so unsatisfactory if the two phenomena – which yet are so obviously interconnected in their real manifestations – could be explained by two different theoretical models to be combined and integrated. But the problem is precisely that these two models, as they flow from the previous theory, cannot be combined, because they are based on different hypotheses about the same dynamic mechanism, and therefore are mutually exclusive.[16]

Let us not be misled on the subject by the way in which the various authors have tried to avoid the problem. Indeed, almost all trade-cycle theorists, after developing their theories with reference to a stationary state, have pointed out that the cyclical mechanism would remain the same if, in the place of a stationary state, a rising trend were introduced. But the trouble is that this *trend* cannot be explained by the same theory

[15] A brilliant criticism of this weak aspect of the present theory can be found in N. Kaldor, 'The Relation of Economic Growth and Cyclical Fluctuations', *The Economic Journal*, 1954, pp. 53–71.

[16] I shall point out that, from this point of view, the macro-economic models under consideration are even less satisfactory than some of the previous theories. For example, in Schumpeter's analysis, the problem outlined in the text does not arise at all, as his theory is such that economic growth can come about only through fluctuations (J. Schumpeter, *The Theory of Economic Development*, Cambridge, Mass., 1934; and *Business Cycles*, 2 vols., New York, 1939).

and, therefore, has to be introduced *ad hoc*. It has to be accepted as given, or justified with supplementary arguments of a nature which must be different from, or independent of, the previous theory. These justifications might quite well be plausible, but the point is that they have to be accepted as such and cannot be derived from the previous theory.

In an analogous but opposite way, the problem has been faced by the theorists of growth, and Duesenberry provides a clear example of it. The same behavioural dynamic mechanism, which has been used by the previous authors in order to explain the cycles, is used in this case in order to explain growth, by relying on different values of the parameters. In so doing, of course, one can no longer explain cycles and therefore the only thing that remains is to rely on a periodical non-satisfaction of the conditions of steady growth, by supposing that some external causes bring about some sort of interruption. The procedure emerges, therefore, as exactly symmetrical to the one considered above. The same identical dynamic process resulting from the interaction between the multiplier and the accelerator is used, but it is used in order to explain a steady growth. Then, some *ad hoc* interruptions of such a movement are introduced, which are accepted as given or justified by supplementary explanations.[17]

[17] [To the conclusion drawn in this section, namely that the multiplier–accelerator mechanism can explain *either* fluctuations *or* growth but not both, the objection has been made that the argument depends on having used a model of difference equations of the second order. It has been suggested that, if a further time lag were introduced in the consumption and/or in the investment function so as to obtain a third order difference equation, then such an equation would have three roots. If one of these were real, positive and greater than unity (but not too much greater than unity) and the other two were conjugate complex, then one could obtain a movement of fluctuating growth. (See, for example, H. Neisser, 'Cyclical Fluctuations and Economic Growth', *Oxford Economic Papers*, 1961, p. 221.)

But this way of presenting the problem is erroneous. Given a particular movement which one wants to obtain (in this case fluctuations around a growing path), of course one can always construct an equation that produces it. Indeed one can go much further. Given any arbitrary succession of points through time, one can always find an algebraic equation of sufficiently high order that will fit the data perfectly. But the artificiality of this procedure precisely consists in having to rely on those very particular values of the parameters that fit the preassigned data.

The problem at issue here is another one, namely: can the differential equation representing the multiplier–accelerator interaction, *in general*, (and independently of the number of time lags) explain a movement of fluctuating growth? The answer is no. The solution of such a differential equation will contain as many roots as the order of its characteristic equation. No matter how many such roots may be, only one of them (or only one pair of conjugate complex roots) will eventually dominate all the others. And the shape of the dominating path will indeed crucially depend on the values of the parameters. In any case, it will be either a path of exponential growth or a path of cyclical fluctuations].

## 9. *A more flexible use of macro-economic models*

Returning now to our main trend of thought, we may notice that the starting point of all criticisms which have been developed in the foregoing sections may be essentially reduced to one point, namely to the excessive degree of confidence that all authors mentioned have ended up by putting in the investment function, the parameters of which are responsible for a radically different behaviour of the system according to the range of values they fall in. This is surprising because no economist would be prepared to rely very much on the stability over time of these parameters, which are well known as particularly sensitive to any kind of change in entrepreneurial expectations.

Now, if the parameters expressing the behaviour of entrepreneurs in their decisions to invest are bound to take different values in time, the situation certainly cannot be solved – as trade-cycle and growth theorists have practically done – by choosing arbitrarily particular values of such parameters and then carrying on one's analysis on the assumption that such values remain constant. If such values do change, we cannot but accept the fact, and go on to a more flexible interpretation of the whole problem.

In fact, there is no reason to suppose that the aggregate behavioural parameters, as time goes on, may not fall from the growth range into the fluctuation range, owing to various causes, and later come back again on a (presumably different) growth path. In this way the various macro-economic models may help us to understand what happens in correspondence to certain particular conditions of entrepreneurial behaviour. If, in addition to this, we consider the natural limitations to growth and the possibility of external 'shocks', we obtain a rather comprehensive view of possible movements corresponding to the various ranges of values within which the initial conditions and the parameters of the investment function may fall.

This is the maximum point to which the macro-economic theories can take us. In this way, however, they come to pose a big problem; the problem of providing a theory which explains the change of the parameters themselves and of the initial conditions which enter into the theoretical framework under consideration. But this is a problem which cannot be solved in the context of a macro-economic analysis, owing to the inherent character of the approach which has been taken. Indeed, in a mathematical formulation, *variables* and *parameters* are taken respectively to denote quantities which are varying and have to be explained, and quantities which are supposed to be constant and given.

Now, if we come to the conclusion that the parameters themselves are changing, then our initial set of assumptions is evidently no longer sufficient.

In our case, if we want to enquire into the causes of variation of those quantities which represent the behavioural parameters of the investment function, we have to widen the theoretical construction from which we started. This means that we have to abandon the macro-economic approach and push our analysis more deeply behind the aggregate parameters themselves, in order to enquire into their *composition*, and in order to single out the different causes – if there are any – which are acting separately on their components.

### 10. *A reinterpretation of the complex dynamics of a modern economic system*

The task just outlined at the end of the previous section appears so complex that I do not pretend to deal with it exhaustively in a few pages. I shall give here, however, the essential lines along which I propose to develop a type of analysis which may lead to a new interpretation of the whole complex dynamics of a modern economic system.[18]

To begin with, let me put the theoretical task just sketched out in different terms, namely in terms of a need to overcome the limitations entailed by macro-economic analysis as such. What is alluded to here is the meaning itself of the macro-economic variables which have been used in all previous analyses. Evidently, in order that the use of such variables may be legitimate, they must measure homogeneous quantities over time. Now, the homogeneity condition would be satisfied if the various total quantities were always composed by the same goods in the same proportions as time goes on; in other words, if the total quantities could be considered as measured in terms of a composite unit, or 'basket of goods' of a constant composition through time. The use of macro-economic variables in a dynamic analysis amounts precisely to an implicit acceptance of this hypothesis, the meaning of which – in a process of economic growth – comes down to the assumption that demand is expanding in a proportional way, namely that it is being distributed among the various goods in such a way as to maintain among them the same proportions in time.

An assumption of this type might perhaps come to be close to reality in the case in which the growth possibilities were confined exclusively

[18] [A more detailed version is contained in the author's Ph.D. thesis: '*A Multi-sector Model of Economic Growth*', University of Cambridge, England, 1962].

to increases of population, with constant returns to scale, no change of tastes and no technical progress. But, in such a case, the problem of adapting the behaviour of investments to the potential physical growth of the system would not be difficult to solve. It is true that all movements we have considered would still be *theoretically* possible. However, entrepreneurs would be faced with a situation in which individual incomes and preferences remain constant through time and they would find them out sooner or later. From that point on, the only possibility which we can reasonably expect is that of a steady growth. In other words, given such a hypothetical case, entrepreneurs might make mistakes or have some hesitations at the beginning, with the effect of causing some fluctuations, but after a few cycles they would certainly find out the individual preferences (which remain unchanged through time); that is to say, they would quickly *learn* the behavioural parameters which lead to an equilibrium growth (compatible with the increase of population).

The problem, of course, is that we do not live in a world of this type, as economists, after all, have always been aware. Whether we take the traditional view of limited resources and diminishing returns to scale, or the more modern view of technical progress developing new resources and reversing on the whole – if not in particular branches – the trend of diminishing returns, the picture is always one of a world where the technical conditions of the productive processes are unceasingly changing.

Taking briefly here the term 'technical progress' for all these movements, we can clearly distinguish two aspects of them, in economic terms. On the one hand, changes in productivity, though operating more or less everywhere, are going on at different rates of change in the various sectors of the economic system, causing thereby a continuous variation of the cost (and of the price) structure. On the other hand, the meaning for the community as a whole of all improvements amounts to a continuous growth of real per-capita income (we shall abstract here, for simplicity, from the complications connected with possible changes in the distribution of income).

The second of these aspects has been completely neglected by all macro-economic models and it comes to assume a particular relevance in our analysis. It is, indeed, an inherent characteristic of economic behaviour, already discovered in the past century by E. Engel[19] and re-

---

[19] E. Engel, 'Die Productions- und Consumptionsverhältnisse des Königreichs Sachsen', *Zeitschrift des Statistischen Bureau des Königlich Sächsischen Ministerium des Inneren*, nos. 8 and 9, 22 Nov. 1857.

cently confirmed and insisted upon by all economists who have dealt with quantitative evaluations of demand, that when real per-capita income increases, the tendency of consumers *is not* to distribute the new income *proportionally* among the commodities previously bought, but, on the contrary, to direct the extra demand towards *new* goods. That is to say, at low real incomes, demand is essentially addressed towards commodities which satisfy the fundamental physiological needs of subsistence (mainly food). As income increases, a part of demand begins to be directed towards other goods (clothes, dwellings, durable goods, etc.) and, as income increases further, towards luxury-goods, services of various kinds, and so on.

As a consequence of this behaviour, the relative *composition* of the purchases of consumers varies in time. For the economic system as a whole, the effects are not only that the employment structure changes (relative decrease of employment in agriculture, relative increase in manufacturing, or even more in services, etc.) but also that the *relative composition* of the national product, in real terms, continuously changes; and this as a direct consequence of technical progress.

I have come here to an important point in my line of argument. The non-proportional growth of demand faces entrepreneurs with a big problem, a problem which *would not exist* in the case of a proportional growth of the whole system. The problem consists in finding out those productive branches (always different as income increases) which correspond to the next consumers' preferences in the process of demand expansion caused by an increasing per-capita income. The problem also entails the adaptation process of consumers to higher possibilities of consumption, and is complicated furthermore by the choice that a growing system is continuously facing, between that part of productivity gains which it prefers devoting to higher production and that part which it prefers devoting to leisure (reduction of the working week). Evidently, in the attempts to find out the solution of this complex problem, the entrepreneurs may make mistakes, and in some periods their fears of being mistaken may be higher than in others, resulting in hesitations and postponements of investment projects. At a macro-economic level, the meaning of these mistakes or simply hesitations comes down to a change in the aggregate behavioural parameters of the system. This has decisive effects on the dynamic movements of effective demand.

It has indeed been an important result of the whole macro-economic analysis to show the dynamic cumulative consequences of certain types of aggregate behaviour. Such an analysis has illustrated that a capitalist system, because of its institutional structure, is bound to move in time according to a mechanism (multiplier–accelerator) which gives rise to different cumulative movements according to the values of the behavioural parameters of the investment function. This theoretical framework, however, has not been able (and is *not* able) to give us any explanation of the values and of the changes in time of such parameters. The arguments which have been developed above now provide such an explanation, which can be used to integrate the previous theoretical framework. They provide, so to speak, the missing link in the theoretical construction.

With this integration, an economic system as a whole emerges not so much with the character of a rigid mechanism, but rather with that of a living organism, which continuously learns from past experience and continually faces new problems to be solved. The important point is that these problems are always new. To learn how to expand the various branches of the economy at a certain moment is not enough, because in the next period the expansion will have to take a different path. The process of the emergence of these new problems and of the variation of the aggregate behavioural parameters, with the consequent possibility of fluctuations, is, therefore, a permanent characteristic, inherent in the elements themselves which determine the growth of a modern economic system.

Looked at in this way, cyclical fluctuations and economic growth, far from appearing two opposite or even incompatible phenomena – as indeed they appear from a view which is purely based on macroeconomic models – emerge as two different aspects or outcomes of the same complex and fundamental process – here comprehensively gathered under the label of 'technical progress' – which incessantly motivates the industrial society in which we live.

## *MATHEMATICAL APPENDIX*

1. In the text of the essay I have tried to avoid too lengthy proofs and long mathematical treatments. The whole mathematics which is behind the stated conclusions is, however, set out in full detail in this appendix.

2. To begin with, let me prove that the conditions which must be satisfied in order that curves (III.7)–(III.8) cross each other exactly coincide with the conditions under which the roots of equation (III.14) are real numbers.

In order to get the values of the capital–output ratios and of the rates of growth which correspond to the intersection of the two curves of fig. (III.1), we have to put $r_k = r_y = r$ in (III.7)–(III.8), and solve the system of equations so obtained. The equations become:

$$r^2 - (\alpha + a - 1 - \beta)r - (\alpha + a - 1)\beta + \alpha\beta = 0,$$
$$\beta v^2 - (\alpha + a - 1 + \beta)v + \alpha = 0,$$

and the solutions are:

$$
\begin{aligned}
r_{1,2} &= \tfrac{1}{2}(\alpha + a - 1 - \beta) \\
&\quad \pm \tfrac{1}{2}\sqrt{\{(\alpha + a - 1 - \beta)^2 + 4(\alpha + a - 1)\beta - 4\alpha\beta\}} \\
&= \tfrac{1}{2}(\alpha + a - 1 - \beta) \pm \tfrac{1}{2}\sqrt{\{(\alpha + a - 1 + \beta)^2 - 4\alpha\beta\}};
\end{aligned}
\tag{A.1}
$$

$$
v_{1,2} = \frac{1}{2\beta}(\alpha + a - 1 + \beta) \mp \frac{1}{2\beta}\sqrt{\{(\alpha + a - 1 + \beta)^2 - 4\alpha\beta\}}.
\tag{A.2}
$$

It can be seen now that the expression which appears under the square root of both (A.1)–(A.2) coincides with the expression which appears under the square root of (III.15). This proves the proposition stated at the beginning of this section.

3. Let us now pass to examine the various types of dynamic behaviour which may emerge from equation (III.12) for the variable $Y$. The first question to be investigated is whether the roots of the quadratic equation (III.14) are real or complex. In order that $x_1$, $x_2$ may be real, the term which appears under the square root of (III.15) must not be negative, namely:

$$(\alpha + a + 1 - \beta)^2 \geqslant 4(\alpha + a - a\beta), \tag{A.3}$$

which may also be written as:

$$(\alpha + a - 1 + \beta)^2 \geqslant 4\alpha\beta. \tag{A.4}$$

The left-hand sides of these inequalities are always positive but the signs of the right-hand sides depend on $\beta$. The only thing we can immediately say, therefore, from (A.3) and (A.4) respectively, is that the inequalities are certainly satisfied when $\beta = 0$ and when $\beta \geqslant 1 + \alpha/a$. What happens in between these two limits requires further investigation. Taking the derivatives of both sides of (A.3) with respect to $\beta$, we obtain:

$$-\frac{d}{d\beta}(\alpha + a + 1 - \beta)^2 = 2(\alpha + a + 1 - \beta), \tag{A.5}$$

$$-\frac{d}{d\beta}(4\alpha + 4a - 4a\beta) = 4a. \tag{A.6}$$

Now, (A.5) is greater than (A.6) when $\beta = 0$, but smaller when $\beta = 1 + \alpha/a$. This means that, as $\beta$ increases, the left-hand side of (A.3) decreases faster than the right-hand side until $\beta = (\alpha + 1 - a)$, and slower thereafter. In other words, as $\beta$ increases, the term under the square root of (III.15) becomes smaller and smaller until a certain point, and then it begins to increase. If it ever becomes negative, in the downward movement, then it necessarily returns to be positive at some later point. To find out whether and where this happens, we must solve the equation:

$$(\alpha + a + 1 - \beta)^2 - 4(\alpha + a - a\beta) = 0,$$

namely:

$$\beta^2 - 2(\alpha + 1 - a)\beta + (\alpha + a - 1)^2 = 0,$$

or,

$$\beta_{1,2} = (\alpha + 1 - a) \mp \tfrac{1}{2}\sqrt{\{4(\alpha + 1 - a)^2 - 4(\alpha + a - 1)^2\}}$$
$$= (\alpha + 1 - a) \mp 2\sqrt{\{a(1 - a)\}}.$$

Since $a < 1$, then $\sqrt{\{a(1 - a)\}}$ is a real number. Hence the term under the square root of (III.15) does become negative as $\beta$ increases, and it does so at $\beta = \beta_1$. As $\beta$ goes on increasing, it returns to be positive when $\beta = \beta_2$.

As a conclusion, the roots of equation (III.14) are *real numbers* when:

$$\beta \leqslant (\alpha + 1 - a) - 2\sqrt{\{a(1 - a)\}},$$

and when $\beta \geqslant (\alpha + 1 - a) + 2\sqrt{\{a(1 - a)\}}$. For $\beta$ falling within these two limits, $x_1$ and $x_2$ are *complex numbers*.

4. Let us investigate first of all the case in which $x_1$ and $x_2$ are real numbers, i.e. the case in which $\beta$ is either $\leqslant$ than $(\alpha + 1 - a) - 2\sqrt{\{a(1 - a)\}}$, or $\geqslant$ than $(\alpha + 1 - a) + 2\sqrt{\{a(1 - a)\}}$.

In this case, as can be seen from (III.13), the dynamic movement of $Y_t$ is fundamentally different according as $x_1$ and $x_2$ are positive or negative, smaller or greater than unity. A way of finding this out is to calculate the function:

$$f(x) = x^2 - (\alpha + a + 1 - \beta)x + (\alpha + a - a\beta),$$

for critical values of $x$, namely:

$$f(\infty) = +\infty,$$
$$f(1) = \beta(1 - a),$$
$$f(0) = a + \alpha - a\beta,$$
$$f(-1) = 2(\alpha + a + 1) - \beta(1 + a),$$
$$f(-\infty) = +\infty,$$

$$\text{(A.7)}$$

and to bear in mind that:

$$x_1 + x_2 = (\alpha + a + 1 - \beta). \tag{A.8}$$

Consider first the interval in which $\beta \leqslant (\alpha + 1 - a) - 2\sqrt{\{a(1 - a)\}}$. When exactly $\beta = 0$, all (A.7) are positive except $f(1)$, which is nought. This means that $x = 1$ is, in this case, a root of (III.14). The other root will be $>$ or $<$ than 1 according as to whether $(\alpha + a)$ is $>$ or $<$ than 1. As a corollary, the inequality:

$$(\alpha + a) > 1 \tag{III.17}$$

turns out to be a very important one; it represents a necessary condition for the system to have the larger root $>$ than 1, i.e. to be at all capable of growth. When $0 < \beta \leqslant (\alpha + 1 - a) - 2\sqrt{\{\alpha(1 - a)\}}$, all (A.7) and also (A.8) are positive, which means that both roots are positive. Provided that (III.17) is satisfied, it can be seen immediately from (A.8) that both $x_1$ and $x_2$ are $>$ than 1.

Consider now the second range of values for $\beta$, i.e. the interval in which:

$$\beta \geqslant (\alpha + 1 - a) + 2\sqrt{\{\alpha(1 - a)\}}.$$

When exactly $\beta = (\alpha + 1 - a) + 2\sqrt{\{\alpha(1 - a)\}}$, $x_1$ and $x_2$ are both equal to $[a - \sqrt{\{\alpha(1 - a)\}}]$, which is $<$ than 1. For higher values of $\beta$, a further distinction has to be made. If $\alpha < a^2/(1 - a)$, there exists an interval in which $\beta$ is $>$ than $(\alpha + 1 - a) + 2\sqrt{\{\alpha(1 - a)\}}$ but $<$ than $(\alpha + a + 1)$, the last expression representing the value of $\beta$ at which $x_1 + x_2 = 0$. It appears from (A.7) and (A.8) that within such an interval the roots are both $<$ than 1, either both positive (when $f(0) > 0$), or one positive and one negative but $x_1 > |x_2|$, (when $f(0) < 0$). If $\alpha > a^2/(1 - a)$, such an interval does not exist and for:

$$(\alpha + a + 1) < \beta < 2(\alpha + a + 1)/(1 + a),$$

it appears again from (A.7) and (A.8) that the real roots are both $<$ than 1 in absolute value, either both negative – when $f(0) > 0$ – or one positive and one negative but $x_1 < |x_2|$ – when $f(0) < 0$. Finally, when

$$\beta > 2(\alpha + a + 1)/(1 + a),$$

the ranges for the two roots are $1 > x_1 > 0$ and $x_2 < -1$.

5. As a result of the foregoing analysis, we can trace the dynamic behaviour of $Y_t$ which emerges from (III.13) when the roots of (III.14) are real. Both $x_1$ and $x_2$ contribute to the movement in time of $Y_t$ but *eventually* only the larger of the two will dominate, in the sense that it will practically determine by itself alone the dynamic movement of $Y_t$.

Therefore, supposing for the time being that the arbitrary constants are positive and that (III.17) is satisfied, when $\beta$ is in the first of the two ranges of values stated at the beginning of the previous section, i.e. when

$$\beta \leqslant (\alpha + 1 - a) - 2\sqrt{\{\alpha(1 - a)\}},$$

the higher root is $>$ than 1, and, therefore, after a few periods, $Y_t$ will grow exponentially at a percentage rate of growth which in time approaches the value:

$$\tfrac{1}{2}(\alpha + a - 1 - \beta) + \tfrac{1}{2}\sqrt{\{(\alpha + a + 1 - \beta)^2 - 4(\alpha + a - a\beta)\}}.$$

When $\beta$ is in the second range of real roots, the movements are more complicated. So long as $(\alpha + 1 - a) + 2\sqrt{\{\alpha(1 - a)\}} \leqslant \beta < (\alpha + a + 1)$, the higher root in absolute value is positive and $<$ than 1, so that $Y_t$ diminishes in time approaching zero asymptotically. When

$$(\alpha + a + 1) < \beta < 2(\alpha + a + 1)/(1 + a)$$

(i.e. when the larger root is negative and $<$ than 1 in absolute value), $Y_t$ oscillates abruptly from positive to negative values and vice versa from one period to another but the oscillations die out as time goes on. Finally, when $\beta > 2(\alpha + a + 1)/(1 + a)$ (i.e. when the larger root is negative and $>$ than 1 in absolute value), $Y_t$ oscillates as in the previous case but in an explosive way. The last two cases represent, indeed, very peculiar movements of the system. Fortunately, they do not have any relevant economic meaning, because, in order to come into existence, they would require a very high and unrealistic value for the parameter $\beta$. More precisely, if we recall here the interpretation which has been given in section 2 of the essay, these movements would require an investment function such as to make the adaptation of the stock of capital to any variation of income at least twice as fast as the adaptation of consumption to the same variation of income. This is extremely unrealistic.

6. The relation between $\beta$ and the roots of equation (III.14) can better be grasped by a graphical representation[20]. Take equation (III.14) and write it in the following way:

$$\frac{1}{a - x}\,[x^2 - (\alpha + a + 1)x + (\alpha + a)] = \beta.$$

By now plotting $x$ on the abscissa and $\beta$ on the ordinate, we obtain a hyperbola with centre at $[a, (1 - a + \alpha)]$ and asymptotes represented by the straight lines $a - x = 0$ and $x + \beta - (1 + \alpha) = 0$. Since all our parameters are greater than zero and $a < 1$, it follows that the centre and at least a stretch of each of the two branches of the hyperbola always fall in the positive quadrant. A graphical representation is given in fig. III.3, where the following values have been assumed for the parameters: $a = 0.85$, $\alpha = 0.75$.

We can now see immediately the relation between $x$ and $\beta$. For any predetermined value of $\beta$, the roots $x_1$ and $x_2$ of (III.14) correspond (from right to left) to the points at which the straight line parallel to the abscissa, and cutting the ordinate at the predetermined value of $\beta$, intersects the hyperbola. (In fig. III.3 one of such straight lines has been drawn corresponding to $\beta = \bar{\beta}$.) Such intersections, as can be seen from fig. III.3, take place at two points (two solutions) in the regions where:

$$\beta < (\alpha + 1 - a) - 2\,\sqrt{\{\alpha(1 - a)\}},$$

and where $\beta > (\alpha + 1 - a) + 2\sqrt{\{\alpha(1 - a)\}}$. They take place at a single point (case in which $x_1$ and $x_2$ coincide) at the extremes of the mentioned inequalities, and at no point at all in the region which is within these two extremes. This last region corresponds to the interval (to be examined later) where the roots $x_1$ and $x_2$ are complex.

[20] The idea has been suggested to me by Professor Carlo Felice Manara.

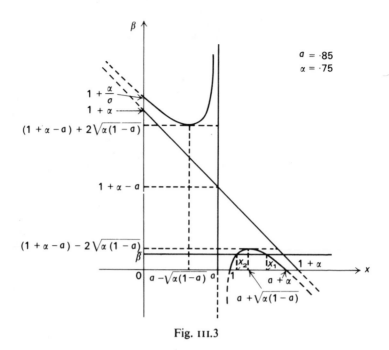

Fig. III.3

7. After examining the movements of $Y_t$ in the case of real roots, it now becomes easy to derive the corresponding movements of $K_t$. By substituting (III.13) into (III.11) and using (III.14), we obtain:

$$K_t = v_1 A_1 x_1{}^t + v_2 A_2 x_2{}^t, \qquad (\text{III.19})$$

where:

$$v_1 = \frac{\alpha + a - x_1}{\beta} = \frac{1}{2\beta}(\alpha + a + \beta - 1)$$

$$- \frac{1}{2\beta}\sqrt{\{(\alpha + a + 1 - \beta)^2 - 4(\alpha + a - a\beta)\}},$$

$$v_2 = \frac{\alpha + a - x_2}{\beta} = \frac{1}{2\beta}(\alpha + a + \beta - 1) \qquad (\text{A.9})$$

$$+ \frac{1}{2\beta}\sqrt{\{(\alpha + a + 1 - \beta)^2 - 4(\alpha + a - a\beta)\}}.$$

As can be seen, the variable $K_t$ depends exactly on the same initial conditions ($A_1$ and $A_2$) and on the same exponential functions ($x_1{}^t$ and $x_2{}^t$) on which $Y_t$ depends. Moreover, it depends on the constants $v_1$ and $v_2$. We may now write (A.9) in a more convenient way, namely:

$$v_1 = \frac{1}{2\beta}(\alpha + a + \beta - 1) - \frac{1}{2\beta}\sqrt{\{(\alpha + a + \beta - 1)^2 - 4\alpha\beta\}},$$

$$v_2 = \frac{1}{2\beta}(\alpha + a + \beta - 1) + \frac{1}{2\beta}\sqrt{\{(\alpha + a + \beta - 1)^2 - 4\alpha\beta\}},$$
(A.10)

where the expressions appearing under the square roots are positive by hypothesis (we are considering the case in which $x_1$ and $x_2$ are real). Therefore, when (III.17) is satisfied, the $v_1$ and $v_2$ are *positive*. They correspond exactly to the (A.2).

As a conclusion, when the roots are real, the behaviour of $K_t$ in time is of the same type as the behaviour of $Y_t$, i.e. it may take all movements already described in section 5, in correspondence to the already stated intervals for the parameter $\beta$.

8. A very interesting economic meaning for the constants $v_1$ and $v_2$ emerges from the model by considering the dynamic movement of the ratio of $K_t$ to $Y_t$. From (III.13) and (III.19), we may write:

$$\frac{K_t}{Y_t} = \frac{v_1 A_1 x_1{}^t + v_2 A_2 x_2{}^t}{A_1 x_1{}^t + A_2 x_2{}^t}.$$

Supposing now that $|x_1| > |x_2|$ and dividing both numerator and denominator by $x_1{}^t$, we obtain:

$$\frac{K_t}{Y_t} = \frac{v_1 A_1 + v_2 A_2 (x_2/x_1)^t}{A_1 + A_2 (x_2/x_1)^t},$$

where, as $t \to \infty$, $(x_2/x_1)^t \to 0$ and $K_t/Y_t \to v_1$. This means that, as time goes on, the ratio $K_t/Y_t$ tends asymptotically to a well-defined value which – in the case of $|x_1| > |x_2|$ – is represented by the constant $v_1$.

Analogously, when $|x_2| > |x_1|$, $(K_t/Y_t) \to v_2$.

9. We have not so far examined the signs of the constants $A_1$ and $A_2$. In sections 5–8 we have simply supposed that they are positive. The time has now come to look more deeply into this matter. If we assume that capital and income at time zero are given, and if we call them by $K_0$ and $Y_0$, we obtain the values of $A_1$ and $A_2$ by putting $t = 0$ in (III.13) and (III.19). We have:

$$Y_0 = A_1 + A_2,$$
$$K_0 = v_1 A_1 + v_2 A_2,$$

and therefore:

$$A_1 = (v_2 Y_0 - K_0)/(v_2 - v_1),$$
(III.21)

$$A_2 = (K_0 - v_1 Y_0)/(v_2 - v_1).$$
(III.22)

The denominators of (III.21)–(III.22) are always positive, since $v_2 > v_1$, but the numerators are positive only when, respectively, $(K_0/Y_0) < v_2$ and $(K_0/Y_0) > v_1$. In any case, only one of the constants $A_1$, $A_2$ (the one entering the dominant term) becomes eventually relevant in (III.13) and (III.19). From our previous analysis we know that the case which has an economic meaning is the case in which $x_1$ is the higher root in absolute value, and therefore $A_1$ becomes the relevant constant. In this case, (III.21) now shows that $A_1$ might happen to be negative. Therefore, the dynamic behaviour of $Y_t$ and $K_t$ are as they have been described in section 5 only if the system starts from a situation where $(K_0/Y_0) < v_2$. In this case, the ratio $K_t/Y_t$ will tend to $v_1$ as time goes on. But if the system starts from a position in which $(K_0/Y_0) > v_2$, and therefore $A_1$ does turn out to be negative, a very different behaviour of the system comes into being. Both $Y_t$ and $K_t$ will eventually either explode negatively (if $x_1 > 1$) or converge to zero from the negative side (if $x_1 < 1$), while the capital–output ratio will still tend to a positive value $v_1$, but with negative numerator and denominator. In these two cases of negative $A_1$, however, our type of analysis has only a hypothetical relevance, because what matters practically is no longer how the system will behave eventually but how it behaves in the first few periods (when the larger root is not necessarily dominating). Afterwards, some physical limits will soon put in check the endogenous forces of the system and our equations will lose any interpretative value.

The other case which remains to be considered – i.e. the case in which $|x_2| > |x_1|$ and therefore $A_2$ becomes the constant of the dominant term – has no relevant economic meaning, as has already been pointed out. In this case, a negative sign for $A_2$ does not change qualitatively the already-described behaviour of $K_t$ and $Y_t$ (namely violent oscillations from negative to positive values and vice versa). The capital–output ratio still tends towards a positive value ($v_2$ this time) but with numerator and denominator both oscillating in sign from period to period.

10. We come at last to tackle the case in which $x_1$ and $x_2$ are complex numbers. In this case, expression (III.13) comes to be composed by real parts and by imaginary parts, so that it is not suitable for a quick investigation. Fortunately, when $x_1$ and $x_2$ are *complex*, they also have the property of being *conjugate*, as can be seen from (III.15). This enables us to use a well-known device for transforming (III.13). In this case, by hypothesis:

$$(\alpha + a + 1 - \beta)^2 - 4(\alpha + a - a\beta) < 0.$$

We can use the notations:

$$d = \tfrac{1}{2}(\alpha + a + 1 - \beta),$$
$$g = \tfrac{1}{2}\sqrt{\{-[(\alpha + a + 1 - \beta)^2 - 4(\alpha + a - a\beta)]\}},$$
$$i = \sqrt{(-1)},$$

and write (III.13) as:

$$Y_t = A_1(d + ig)^t + A_2(d - ig)^t.$$

This expression may be written in terms of trigonometric functions, namely[21]:

$$Y_t = B\rho^t \cos(t\theta + \varepsilon), \tag{III.16}$$

where the arbitrary constants (to be determined, in our problem, by initial conditions) are now $B$ and $\cos \varepsilon$. The other terms are related to the original parameters of our system by the following definitions:

$$\rho = \sqrt{(\alpha + a - a\beta)}, \tag{A.11}$$

$$\cos \theta = \frac{\alpha + a + 1 - \beta}{2\sqrt{[\alpha + a - a\beta]}}. \tag{A.12}$$

11. Expression (III.16) is equivalent to (III.13) and has the advantage, when $x_1$ and $x_2$ are complex, of being expressed entirely in real terms. It is now easy to infer from it the dynamic behaviour of $Y_t$ in the case of complex roots. As $t$ increases, the cos term in (III.16) brings about regular cycles of a constant length, approximately equal to $360°/\theta$ periods of time. The amplitude and the phase of the first cycle are determined by the constants $B$ and $\cos \varepsilon$. Then, whether the amplitude of successive cycles will become greater or smaller depends on the *modulus* $\rho$. If $\rho > 1$, the amplitude will increase (explosive cycles); if, on the other hand, $\rho < 1$, the amplitude will decrease (damped cycles).

In our problem – as we have seen – the range within which the roots are complex is:

$$(\alpha + 1 - a) - 2\sqrt{\{\alpha(1 - a)\}} < \beta < (\alpha + 1 - a) + 2\sqrt{\{\alpha(1 - a)\}}.$$

By substituting these two extremes into (A.11), it can be seen that, for $\beta$ equal to the first extreme, $\rho$ is more than 1, provided that (III.17) is satisfied, and for $\beta$ equal to the second extreme, $\rho$ is $<$ than 1 (except for exceptional values of $\alpha$, of the order of 100, for $a = 0.85$, in which case $\rho$ remains $>$ than 1). Normally, therefore, there is a value of $\beta$ within the range of complex roots [and this value is $\beta = (\alpha + a - 1)/a$], which divides the range of explosive from the range of damped fluctuations.

12. The expression representing the movement of $K_t$, in the case of complex roots is similar to the one representing the movement of $Y_t$. Substituting from (III.16), equation (III.19) becomes:

$$K_t = \frac{B}{\beta} \rho^t[(\alpha + a) \cos(t\theta + \varepsilon) - \sqrt{(\alpha + a - a\beta)} \cos(t\theta + \varepsilon + \theta)],$$

---

[21] See, for example, Allen, *Mathematical Economics*, ch. 6.

which may usefully be written in a simpler way after a few transformations:

$$K_t = \frac{B}{\beta} \rho^t \{(\alpha + a) \cos (t\theta + \varepsilon) -$$
$$\sqrt{(\alpha + a - a\beta)}[\cos (t\theta + \varepsilon) \cos \theta - \sin (t\theta + \varepsilon) \sin \theta]\},$$

$$K_t = \frac{B}{\beta} \rho^t \{[\alpha + a - \sqrt{(\alpha + a - a\beta)} \cos \theta] \cos (t\theta + \varepsilon)$$
$$+ \sqrt{(\alpha + a - a\beta)} \sin \theta \sin (t\theta + \varepsilon)\}. \tag{A.13}$$

Putting now:

$$\alpha + a - \sqrt{(\alpha + a - a\beta)} \cos \theta = \zeta \cos \eta,$$
$$\sqrt{(\alpha + a - a\beta)} \sin \theta = \zeta \sin \eta,$$

where:

$$\zeta^2 = [\alpha + a - \sqrt{(\alpha + a - a\beta)} \cos \theta]^2 + (\alpha + a - a\beta) \sin^2 \theta,$$

$$\text{tg } \eta = \frac{\sqrt{(\alpha + a - a\beta)} \sin \theta}{\alpha + a - \sqrt{(\alpha + a - a\beta)} \cos \theta},$$

and substituting into (A.13), we come to the expression:

$$K_t = \frac{B}{\beta} \rho^t [\zeta \cos \eta \cos (t\theta + \varepsilon) + \zeta \sin \eta \sin (t\theta + \varepsilon)],$$

which, by an elementary property of trigonometric functions, may finally be written:

$$K_t = \frac{B}{\beta} \zeta \rho^t \cos (t\theta + \varepsilon - \eta). \tag{III.20}$$

The relation between the fluctuations of capital and the fluctuations of income can now be directly inferred by a comparison of (III.20) with (III.16). The cycle of $K_t$ is related to the cycle of $Y_t$ by a fixed proportion ($\gamma = \zeta/\beta$), it has exactly the same length (360/θ periods of time) and the same behaviour over time (determined by ρ), but a different phase, in the sense that it lags behind it by a fraction η/θ of a period of time. The same constants $B$ and cos ε determine the amplitude and the phase of the first fluctuation.

13. We may finally have a look again at the case in which the system produces a steady growth, in order to find out the factors which determine the proportional rate of change. The topic is relevant for the discussion which is carried out in section 7 of the essay.

We have seen already that a steady (exponential) growth takes place when $0 \leqslant \beta \leqslant (\alpha + 1 - a) - 2\sqrt{\{\alpha(1 - a)\}}$. We may notice now that the second extreme of this interval can never be negative, since:

$$\alpha + (1 - a) - 2\sqrt{\{\alpha(1 - a)\}} = [\alpha^{\frac{1}{2}} - (1 - a)^{\frac{1}{2}}]^2 \geqslant 0.$$

## Fluctuations and economic growth

It follows that there normally exists a whole family of positive $\beta$ which leads to a steady growth.

For any given $\beta$ belonging to this family, the rate of growth of the system depends on the value of $\alpha$ relatively to the value of $a$, as can be seen immediately from the expression we have found (in section 5 of this appendix) for the proportional rate of growth of the system (which we may call $g$), namely from:

$$g = \tfrac{1}{2}[\alpha - (1 - a) - \beta] + \tfrac{1}{2}\sqrt{\{(\alpha + a + 1 - \beta)^2 - 4(\alpha + a - a\beta)\}}.$$
$$(\text{A.}14)$$

The simplest way of considering (A.14) is to begin by supposing that $\beta$ takes the maximum value allowed by the exponential growth range. In such a case, the expression which appears under the square root of (A.14) vanishes, and the proportional rate of growth of the system becomes:

$$g = \tfrac{1}{2}[\alpha - (1 - a) - \beta].$$
$$(\text{A.}15)$$

We can see from (A.15) that for any predetermined $a$ and $\beta$, $g$ may take any large or small value as we like depending entirely on the value of $\alpha$. The same proposition remains valid (with the difference that higher values of $g$ will correspond to the same values of $\alpha$) for any value of $\beta$ which is lower than the maximum.

# IV

# From Classical to Keynesian economic dynamics

It has been mentioned above[1] that, alongside that group of Keynesian theories which have tried to interpret the actual movements of national income (and employment) through time, another group of theories has been developed which has been more simply aimed at stating the conditions for steady growth. The foundations of these theories are best seen by going back to our previous analysis of Essay II, where three major shortcomings of Ricardo's theory have been mentioned, but only one of them has been considered (effective demand). In the present essay the picture will be completed by considering the other two, concerning population growth and technical progress. We have seen that, on effective demand, other authors in Ricardo's time (especially Malthus and Sismondi) had been able to perceive the problems involved. But on population growth and technical progress Ricardo's pessimistic views were shared by all British economists of his time. The roots of this pessimism are again to be found in Malthus – but in Malthus the population theorist.

## 1. *Pre-Malthusian views on population*

Views on population growth took a striking turn at the end of the eighteenth century, as is well known.

For centuries, basic assumptions on population had very rarely been challenged. In societies which, from a technological point of view, were practically stationary, numbers meant strength and prosperity. Almost everywhere a large population was regarded as a blessing for the Monarch, and for the people themselves, besides contributing to the glory of God.

This was still the prevalent opinion at the times of Adam Smith, who could write, without feeling any need to justify it, that 'The most

---

[1] Essay III, p. 54.

86

decisive mark of the prosperity of any country is the increase of the number of its inhabitants.'[2] But Adam Smith introduced something new, by forcibly insisting on the improvement of productivity, through division of labour, as the major cause of the wealth of a nation, irrespective of its endowments of natural resources.[3] The modernity of this view is really extraordinary. Adam Smith was the first economist to perceive clearly the great possibilities that had come to light with the application of technological advance to the process of production (i.e. with the Industrial Revolution). Population growth could not but be complementary to technical progress.

All of a sudden, however, at the end of the century, the general view began to change. Various authors became preoccupied with the pressure that a large population can impose on resources.[4] Especially in England, population had been increasing as never before; and this was taken as an immediate effect of industrialization. The general mood quickly became receptive to new ideas; and when, in 1798, Malthus published his concise and clearly argued 'Essay' on population he had an astounding success. Thomas Robert Malthus, 'the first of the Cambridge economists'[5]

---

[2] Adam Smith, *An Inquiry into the Nature and Causes of the Wealth of Nations*, ed. by E. Cannan, 2 vols., London, 1904, vol. 1, p. 72.

[3] At the very beginning of his work, Adam Smith states that the 'proportion [of the produce] to the number of those who are to consume it [i.e. per capita – income in modern terminology] ... must in every nation be regulated by two different circumstances; first, by the skill, dexterity and judgment with which its labour is generally applied; and, secondly, by the proportion between the number of those who are employed in useful labour, and that of those who are not so employed. Whatever be the soil, climate or extent of territory of any particular nation, the abundance or scantiness of its annual supply must, in that particular situation, depend upon those two circumstances.' (Adam Smith, *The Wealth of Nations*, pp. 1, 2.) The Classical view of the causes of the wealth of a nation stands out clearly in this remarkable passage, in striking contrast with the later 'marginal productivity' view, which relies entirely on resource endowments and neglects the improvements in productivity.

[4] Detailed reviews may be found in James Bonar, *Theories of Population from Raleigh to Arthur Young*, London, 1931; and in C. E. Stangeland, *Pre-Malthusian Doctrines of Population*, New York, 1904. It seems that the first writer ever to suggest a possible conflict between population growth and means of subsistence was the Italian Giovanni Botero (1589). The 'law of geometric progression' was stated later by W. Petty (1686), J. P. Süssmilch (1740) and R. Wallace (1753). The Venetian economist, Giammaria Ortes, went much further in his *Riflessioni sulla popolazione delle nazioni per rapporto all'economia nazionale*, written between 1775 and 1787, and published in 1790. He stated both the geometric progression of population, as opposed to the slower increase of food, and the desirability of checks through celibacy and 'reason'.

[5] The epithet is Keynes', who used it as a sub-title to his essay on Malthus, in *Essays in Biography*, London, 1933.

was then to become a 'professor of history and political economy', but his views on economic theory were to remain unsuccessful. His name reigns supreme in the history of theories of population.

## 2. *Malthus' principle of population*

The full title of the first edition of Malthus' famous work is 'An Essay on the Principle of Population, as it affects the future Improvement of Society, with Remarks on the Speculations of Mr. Godwin, M. Condorcet, and other Writers'. Its origin is curious. Malthus had been disputing with his father on 'the general question of the improvement of society' and in particular on the state of perfection of society cherished by Godwin and Condorcet.[6] As against these writers, Malthus wanted to contend the impossibility of society ever being able to arrive at perfection. He started from the proposition that checks to the growth of population produce 'misery and vice', and went on to prove that checks are necessary. To this effect he developed what he came to call 'the principle of population'. This principle simply states that population grows naturally according to a geometric progression, but the means of subsistence can only be made to grow according to an arithmetic progression. Hence the inevitability of checks to population growth. Malthus could conclude that since checks imply 'misery and vice', and since checks are necessary, perfectibility is impossible. It is, however, the 'principle of population' that immediately became famous, not Malthus' arguments against the perfectibility of society. In the second edition of the book, the perfectibility arguments were dropped and the principle of population was presented for its own sake.[7]

Critics of Malthus have since pointed out that there is no reason why, if population increases exponentially, the means of subsistence should increase only arithmetically. After all, 'God sends a pair of hands with every mouth', as the proverb says, and moreover new and better methods of cultivation are continually implemented, through division of labour

[6] See Malthus' Preface to the first edition of his *Essay*, and J. Bonar, *Malthus and his Work*, London, 1924, pp. 6 ff.

[7] It has been quite well documented by now that the first edition (1798) of Malthus' *Essay* and its second edition (1803) are two quite different works. The first edition is a 50,000-word short essay. The second edition is four times as long as the first, and contains only a fraction of what is in the first. The full title of the second edition reads: 'An Essay on the Principle of Population; or, a View of its Past and Present Effects on Human Happiness; with an Inquiry into our Prospects respecting the Future Removal or Mitigation of the Evils which it Occasions'. It is in this edition that Malthus introduces 'moral restraint' or virtuous abstention from marriage as a further check to population.

and better technical knowledge. But it is precisely on this point – on the relative importance of population growth and technical progress – that Malthus had a deep conviction. He was convinced that, in spite of any technical improvement, the growth of population would inevitably be more rapid than the growth of production. His arguments, however, were not at all stringent. As Edwin Cannan has carefully pointed out, Malthus' arguments were basically sound on population growing exponentially, but were very feeble indeed on the means of subsistence only being able to grow according to an arithmetical progression.[8] The intellectual environment in England at the end of the eighteenth century was, however, favourably receptive to Malthus' conviction. And there the matter rested.

It must be pointed out that, had the problem been left in these terms, it would have been easy, after all, to reverse Malthus' view as soon as historical evidence had shown the opposite. For, whether the produce per man increases or decreases with the growth of population is a matter for empirical evidence. But this is not how matters developed. Once Malthus' conviction gained ground, it was backed up by more complicated (and thus more prestigious) arguments, which took the shape of a newly discovered economic law – the 'law of diminishing returns'.

### 3. *The 'law of diminishing returns'*

The law of diminishing returns on land was presented almost simultaneously, within the space of twenty-one days, in an eventful February 1815, by no less than four leading English economists: Malthus, West, Ricardo and Torrens.[9] The circumstances are interesting. The House of Lords and the House of Commons had appointed committees to enquire into the causes of the extremely high price of corn over the previous twenty years, and of the unpopularly high rents on land (the famous 'corn question'). More than one landowner defended the situation by claiming that the improvement of cultivation required an increasing number of enclosures of poorer land, on which rent was very low in spite of the high price of corn; and that a diminution of prices, or importation of corn at lower prices, would stop improvement in agriculture and cause disruption in capital employed on the least fertile lands.[10] Within a few weeks from publication of the enquiry, the leading

[8] Edwin Cannan, *A History of the Theories of Production and Distribution*, 2nd ed., London, 1903, pp. 130 ff.

[9] See the meticulous reconstruction of the events made by Piero Sraffa in vol. IV, pp. 3–8 of *The Works and Correspondence of David Ricardo*, Cambridge, 1951.

[10] See the detailed account given by Cannan, *op. cit.*, pp. 147 ff.

economists of the time produced their generalization: a universal 'law of diminishing returns'.

The expedient was a very elegant one; for, it enabled them to put a scientific 'law' behind the Malthusian principle of population, and at the same time to enunciate a theory of increasing rents. They could state that, as the number of people increases, it is true that a pair of hands comes with every mouth, but while the new mouths require as much food as the old ones, the new hands produce less and less, by being employed on less and less fertile lands or on more intensively exploited lands. The price of the agricultural produce could not but increase, and so would total rent.[11] The increasing rents were thereby presented as the direct consequence of the increasing population.

It should be noted that the law of diminishing returns is not necessary to either the Malthusian principle of population or the Ricardian theory of rent. Malthus had originally enunciated his principle of population without reference to the law of diminishing returns, simply as his view on the relative rapidity of increase of population and of the produce of the earth. And the differential theory of rent (the explanation that rent arises because of the different fertility of various lands, granted that the prices of the products must be the same, independently of whether grown on more or less fertile lands) had already been anticipated very clearly in 1777 by James Anderson, who not only did not link it up with diminishing returns, but actually claimed the opposite (indefinite possibility of improvements).[12] But again, there the matter rested.

The law of diminishing returns became a powerful analytical tool which rendered Malthus' principle of population and Ricardo's gloomy view of the development of a capitalist society almost impregnable to criticism. From the generalization of a particular situation of the corn price in England in the early nineteenth century came a 'law' which has dominated economic theory ever since. Political economy itself, from a science dealing with the causes of the wealth of a nation, had been turned into what, to external observers, could only appear as 'the dismal science'.[13]

[11] This has become known as the 'Ricardian' theory of rent, although West and Malthus should be given more credit for it than Ricardo.

[12] Anderson's anticipation is contained in a much quoted passage from his *Inquiry into the Nature of the Corn Laws*, published in 1777. See: Cannan, *op. cit.*, pp. 371–3. Anderson was arguing in favour of protection so as to force inferior lands into cultivation. He was convinced that these inferior lands would eventually be made as productive as the other (more fertile) lands.

[13] The epithet, attributed to Carlyle, was extensively used in nineteenth-century England.

## 4. *Population growth and technical progress*

Two centuries of economic history of the industrial countries have shown to anybody's eye the importance of population growth and of technical progress in the evolution of modern societies.

As far as population is concerned, there can be no doubt that its unprecedented growth is a very typical phenomenon of the industrial age. That it poses very serious problems to society is no longer disputed today. Nobody, however, would be prepared to accept any longer Malthus' and Ricardo's naïve idea that population is kept back by lack of food, and that any increase of incomes induces workers to reproduce themselves at such a fast rate as to bring their per-capita wages back to where they started from. This may well happen in certain particular circumstances, but the whole problem of the relation of growth of population and changes in per-capita income has turned out to be much more complicated than the Classical economists thought. Modern economists have become a little more modest in this respect and now simply take the movements of population through time as exogenously given. The normal assumption is that population increases at a steady percentage rate of growth.

Technical progress has been a much harder phenomenon to incorporate into economic analysis. This is paradoxical. In a period in history which has witnessed the most surprising and unprecedented advances in technology and their applications to production, the established economic theory has proceeded for more than a century on the amazingly myopic assumption of no change in technical knowledge. So pervasive has been the influence of the law of diminishing returns on the whole way of economic thinking! Even today this 'law' is still haunting economic theorists in all sorts of devious ways. When faced with an increase in production per man, even at the most simplified and pedestrian stage of a one-commodity-world, any economic theorist subservient to tradition will be unable to begin doing anything unless he proceeds first to break down the change into two different types of changes: changes due to a variation of the proportions of 'factors', *at diminishing returns*; and changes due to a 'shift' of the (otherwise assumed to be rigidly fixed in shape) technical functions. He will admit that the second type of change is in the long run so overwhelmingly preponderant as to reduce the first to a very little thing, in comparison.[14]

[14] In a well known empirical study ('Technical Change and the Aggregate Production Function', *The Review of Economics and Statistics*, 1957, pp. 312–20) Robert Solow has investigated the increase of production per man in the U.S. during the

He will moreover, a little more grudgingly, admit that any distinction between the two is widely arbitrary.[15] He will even be compelled to mention that, in fact, it is not actually sure that diminishing returns to changing factor proportions should really take place. In some cases, the opposite happens.[16] But he will call these cases 'perverse' and those that conform to tradition 'well-behaved'. And of course he will not consider perversity but only good behaviour. No surprise that at this point the model has become so complicated as to make it practically impossible ever to go beyond the first simplified stage.

The really decisive step towards modern economic dynamics was taken when Harrod, in a Keynesian (and Ricardian) manner, took important things first and simply reversed Malthus' view. At least as a first approximation, he left aside land and concentrated on labour and capital; he left aside changes in 'factor proportions' and simply assumed that technical progress makes production per man increase through time at a steady percentage rate of growth, quite independently of population growth.

This apparently small step, when added to the assumption of a steady growth of population and to the Keynesian theory of effective demand, immediately brought the investigation back to Classical economic dynamics, at the point where Ricardo had left it. The development of this approach has been surprisingly fruitful. This is in itself a great tribute to Ricardo's genius. The post-Keynesian theories of economic growth and income distribution can be directly grafted on to the Ricardian theoretical framework, as if nothing had happened in between.

---

period 1909–49. By using a traditional production function his conclusion has been that 87·5% of the change is due to a 'shift of the production function' and the remaining 12·5% to an increase in capital intensity (a 'movement along' the production function, with increase in the *proportion* of capital to labour).

[15] See my own discussion with Solow, 'On Concepts and Measures of Changes in Productivity', *The Review of Economics and Statistics*, 1959, pp. 270–86. I have pointed out that, according to Solow's own findings, the aggregate capital–output ratio in the U.S. economy was lower in 1949 than in 1909. It could therefore be argued that, during that period, the overall capital intensity of the U.S. production processes, very far from increasing (as Solow's 'moving along the production function' would suggest), has in fact decreased.

[16] See the discussion on the relation between capital–output ratio and rate of profit, in Essay VI, pp. 132 ff.

## 5. *Long-run equilibrium conditions – Domar's contribution*

The revival of interest in Classical economic dynamics is in itself a direct consequence of Keynes' *General Theory*. Compare Keynes' notion of equilibrium with the traditional notion. In traditional analysis, one may enquire into whether an equilibrium exists, is unique, is stable; and there the matter rests. The achievement of an equilibrium is the end of the story. In Keynesian analysis the opposite is the case. The achievement of full employment equilibrium requires that a certain amount of new investment is undertaken so as to bring total effective demand to the level of full capacity utilization. But the very fact that the appropriate amount of new investment is undertaken comes to change the objective situation (i.e. existing productive capacity) on which current equilibrium is based. In Keynesian analysis, therefore, the very achievement of equilibrium at one particular time, far from being the end of the story, opens up a whole new series of questions on how equilibrium is going to be maintained in the following period. A dynamic analysis becomes inevitable.

It was Domar[17] who began to look at the problem in this way. He pointed out that investments play a strategic role in any economic system, as they act through two quite different channels. On the one side the total level of investment determines the total level of effective demand, through the operation of the multiplier relation:

$$\frac{1}{s} I = Y, \tag{IV.1}$$

where $I$ = new investment, $Y$ = net national income, $s$ = savings to income ratio. On the other side total new investment represents an *addition* to existing productive capacity:

$$\frac{1}{\kappa} I = \frac{dP}{dt}, \tag{IV.2}$$

where $P$ = productive capacity, $\kappa$ = capital–output ratio.[18] (We are considering time $t$ as a continuous variable for analytical simplicity.) Thus while, through (IV.1), investment influences *total* effective demand; through (IV.2), it determines the *increase* of productive capacity. There

[17] E. D. Domar, 'Capital Expansion, Rate of Growth and Employment', *Econometrica*, 1946, pp. 137–47.

[18] I am using here the symbol $\kappa$ to stress the technological character of the capital–output ratio, as against the behavioural character of the parameter $v$ used in Essays II and III.

is, therefore, no reason why these two effects should necessarily be compatible with the maintenance of full capacity utilization.

It becomes necessary to explore the conditions that must be satisfied in order that effective demand and productive capacity may expand *pari passu* through time. Clearly, total effective demand must, first of all, be equal to total productive capacity to begin with, let us say at time zero, i.e.

$$P(0) = Y(0). \tag{IV.3}$$

Secondly the additions to productive capacity, as time goes on, must be always equal to the additions to effective demand, i.e.

$$\frac{dP}{dt} = \frac{dY}{dt}. \tag{IV.4}$$

Supposing that the initial condition (IV.3) is satisfied, equation (IV.4) represents a simple differential equation which, after substitution from (IV.1), (IV.2), becomes:

$$\frac{1}{\kappa} I = \frac{1}{s} \frac{dI}{dt}, \tag{IV.5}$$

from which:

$$\frac{s}{\kappa} dt = \frac{1}{I} dI. \tag{IV.6}$$

By integration and insertion of the initial condition, we obtain the solution:

$$I(t) = I(0) e^{(s/\kappa)t}, \tag{IV.7}$$

where e is the basis of natural logarithms. Expression (IV.7) says that, in order to maintain equilibrium in the long run, i.e. in order to keep productive capacity and effective demand expanding *pari passu*, new investments have to expand through time according to the exponential function specified by (IV.7). The exponent of e in (IV.7) indicates the percentage rate of growth per period considered. We may say therefore that investments must expand at a percentage rate of growth g equal to $s/\kappa$, or:

$$g = \frac{s}{\kappa}. \tag{IV.8}$$

When this happens, net income, consumption and the stock of capital will all grow at the same percentage rate $g$. This is what has become known as the Domar model.

It may be noticed that expression (IV.7), i.e. exponential growth, emerges as the 'solution' to the problem of keeping equilibrium in the long run. Only exponential growth, if $\kappa$ and $s$ remain constant, will keep equality of effective demand and productive capacity through time. It is, moreover, important to realize that the analysis has been carried out at a high level of generality, namely at a pure level of logical consistency. Equality (IV.8) must hold, if long-run equilibrium is to be maintained. It would be misleading to interpret (IV.8) as a description of what is actually happening. Or at least it would be a very inefficient way of interpreting it. (An economy might actually achieve (IV.8), or fail to achieve it, in a variety of different ways. Each one of these ways, in order to be described, would require a whole list of very particular assumptions.) But as an equilibrium condition, i.e. as a condition that must be satisfied for productive capacity to be kept fully utilized, (IV.8) is valid in any case, while requiring a remarkably small number of assumptions – simply constancy of $s$ and $\kappa$. It represents, therefore, a very fundamental relation; so fundamental in fact as to be valid for capitalist and socialist systems alike, i.e. independently of any institutional set-up of society.

## 6. *The 'natural' rate of growth – Harrod's contribution*

By following Keynes too closely, Domar had made no distinction between full utilization of productive capacity and full employment of the labour force (thereby implicitly assuming that they coincide). This would be justified in a short-run analysis (such as Keynes') but is no longer justified as soon as one goes over to the long run. Even supposing that full employment of the labour force and full utilization of productive capacity are realized to begin with, there is no reason to expect that they should continue to be realized as time goes on. This means that Domar's condition (IV.8), though ensuring a *pari passu* growth of effective demand and of productive capacity, does not necessarily ensure maintenance of full employment of the labour force as time goes on. It is at this point that Harrod's[19] contribution may be brought in.

[19] Harrod was the first to find what has now become known as 'the Harrod–Domar equation'; see his 'Essay in Dynamic Theory', *The Economic Journal*, 1939, pp. 14–33. His ideas have been later expounded more completely in his *Towards a Dynamic Economics*, London, 1948.

Suppose that the labour force grows through time according to an exponential function:

$$L(t) = L(0) e^{nt}, \qquad (\text{IV}.9)$$

where: $L(t)$ = labour force at time $t$, and $n$ = percentage rate of growth of the labour force; and suppose that output per man (labour productivity) grows through time according to another exponential function:

$$y(t) = y(0) e^{\lambda t}, \qquad (\text{IV}.10)$$

where: $y(t) = Y(t)/L(t)$ and $\lambda$ = percentage rate of growth of productivity. The sum $g_n$ of the two rates of growth:

$$g_n = n + \lambda, \qquad (\text{IV}.11)$$

has been called by Harrod the 'natural' rate of growth. It represents the maximum sustainable rate of growth that technical conditions make available to the economic system as a whole. If we now call the percentage rate $g$ of equilibrium relation (IV.8) the 'warranted' rate of growth, then we may say that full employment of the labour force and full utilization of productive capacity take place only if:

$$g_n = g, \qquad (\text{IV}.12)$$

i.e. only if the natural rate of growth and the warranted rate of growth are equal to each other. After substitution from (IV.8) we obtain:

$$s = \kappa g_n. \qquad (\text{IV}.13)$$

The saving ratio must be equal to the capital–output ratio multiplied by the natural rate of growth if equilibrium (in the sense of both full employment and full capacity utilization) is to be kept in the long run. It is this relation that has generally become known as the Harrod–Domar equation. It may be noticed that the exponential growth of investment in (IV.7) emerges as a *solution* to the problem of how to keep full employment and full capacity utilization in the long run under constancy conditions of both $\kappa$ and $s$. On the other hand, the exponential growth of the labour force and of productivity is an *assumption*. It may not, therefore, be possible, or it may be only approximately possible, to maintain equilibrium in the long run, if the natural growth of population and of productivity is not exponential, i.e. if $g_n$ is not steady.

Secondly it will be noticed that relation (IV.13), as stated, becomes a very rigid relation indeed. The natural rate of growth $g_n$ is taken as exogenously given and so is $s$. Moreover, Harrod explicitly assumes technical progress to be 'neutral' – defined as such that, at the same rate of interest, the capital–output ratio $\kappa$ remains constant.[20] But if $g_n$, $s$, $\kappa$ are all constant, then relation (IV.13) can only be satisfied by a fluke. Harrod himself prefers to keep this relation in this way. He wants to go on to use his model to describe the actual behaviour of a capitalist system. For this purpose he defines the 'warranted' rate of growth in behaviouristic terms – a rate of growth at 'which producers will be content with what they are doing'.[21] Then from the fact that the 'warranted' and the 'natural' rates of growth will normally be different from each other, he tries to figure out what the *actual* rate of growth will be. But there is no necessity to follow Harrod in this. One thing is the use that Harrod himself makes of relation (IV.13) in his theory of how a capitalist system actually behaves (a theory that depends on his particular assumptions on how entrepreneurs react to a divergence of reality from expectations), and another thing is relation (IV.13) considered as an equilibrium condition. This equilibrium condition, as such, is independent of any behavioural assumption and is even independent of institutions. It is this second way of considering the Harrod–Domar equation that has turned out to be most fruitful, although it immediately raises the problem of abandoning the constancy assumption for at least one of the three magnitudes $s$, $\kappa$, $g_n$. For, if (IV.13) is to be an equation, at least one of $s$, $\kappa$, $g_n$ must be considered as a variable.

### 7. *New answer to an old Ricardian problem*

It becomes easy, at this point, to see that if Harrod–Domar hypotheses are inserted into Ricardo's theoretical scheme and proper account is taken of Keynes' effective demand requirements for full employment, we are led back to the old Ricardian problem of income distribution, but with an entirely new answer. Nicholas Kaldor was the first to see this clearly.[22]

The problem may be illustrated best with reference to technical progress only. Suppose that $n = 0$ and $\lambda > 0$, so that $g_n = \lambda > 0$. For example, we may imagine that the economic system – after arriving at the Ricardian stationary state, where wages are at their 'natural' level and profits are at their minimum – starts enjoying growth of productivity, while population remains absolutely constant. (We shall

---

[20] *Ibid.*, pp. 22–3.     [21] *Ibid.*, p. 81.

[22] N. Kaldor, 'Alternative Theories of Distribution', *The Review of Economic Studies*, 1955–6, pp. 83–100.

abstract from rents.) We may keep Ricardo's assumption that workers spend all their wages on consumption goods, while capitalists save a large fraction of their incomes (profits). If we call $s_w$ and $s_c$, respectively, the propensities to save of the workers and of the capitalists, this means $s_w = 0$ and $s_c > 0$.

We may now ask what will happen to income distribution, if full employment is to be kept through time. Ricardo's answer – although he never explicitly considered this case – would have been that, since wages are stuck at their 'natural' level, all the surplus over wages will be appropriated by the capitalists, who will therefore reap the benefits of technical progress. In other words, that wages will remain constant and profits (and the rate of profit, and the share of profit in total income) will all increase. But this is precisely what Keynes' contribution now enables us to say cannot happen. The reason is provided by the requirements of full-employment effective demand. If the capitalists were to try to appropriate the whole surplus, the economic system would be precipitated into a slump.

Let us consider the problem in detail. The Harrod–Domar equilibrium condition, which we may write:

$$s = \frac{S}{Y} = \kappa\, g_n, \qquad (\text{IV}.14)$$

(where $S$ = total savings) says that the proportion of income that is saved cannot be lower than $\kappa\, g_n$. But it cannot be higher either. This implies that, since $S = s_c P$, where $P$ = total profits, then:

$$\frac{P}{Y} = \frac{1}{s_c}\,\kappa\, g_n. \qquad (\text{IV}.15)$$

The share of profit in national income (besides being required not to be lower) cannot be higher than $(1/s_c)\,\kappa\, g_n$. For, if $(P/Y) > (1/s_c)\,\kappa\, g_n$, then $(S/Y) > \kappa\, g_n$ – i.e. there would be a tendency to excess savings, there would be lack of effective demand and therefore Keynesian unemployment. The only way to preserve full employment in the long run is to let wages rise.

It may be noticed that, since in equilibrium $\kappa = K/Y$, from (IV.15) we obtain:

$$\frac{P}{K} = \frac{1}{s_c}\, g_n, \qquad (\text{IV}.16)$$

which represents the long-run equilibrium rate of profit, in the same way as (IV.15) represents the long-run equilibrium share of profit. It may also be noticed that this treatment of income distribution

98

implicitly provides a way out of the Harrod–Domar *impasse* over the rigidity of relation (IV.13). For, although the propensities to save $s_w$ and $s_c$ are constant, the aggregate savings to income ratio $S/Y$ becomes a variable, through changes in income distribution.

The conclusion is that if $s_c$, $\kappa$ and $g_n$ remain constant in time, maintainance of full employment in the long run requires a constant rate of profit and a constant distribution of income between profits and wages; and therefore requires growth of wages and of the wage-rate. In the case considered here, both total wages and the wage-rate must increase at the same rate of growth as productivity. After profits have provided for capital accumulation and capitalists' consumption, the benefits of technical progress accrue to the workers.

## 8. *Kaldor's theory of income distribution*

Kaldor has actually carried out his analysis on the slightly more general assumptions that $n > 0$ and $s_w > 0$, where, $s_w < (I/Y) < s_c$.[23]

[23] N. Kaldor, *Review of Economic Studies*, 1955–6. Kaldor calls his theory of distribution 'Keynesian' (by referring to a passage in Keynes' *Treatise on Money*, London 1931, p. 139), although Keynes never stated it explicitly. But more than Keynes, a notable precursor of Kaldor is perhaps Michal Kalecki, who was however interested in short-run situations and tended to emphasize the role of the degree of monopoly. Kalecki worked on the assumption that all wages are spent (i.e. workers' propensity to save is zero) and that profits are partly saved and partly consumed. On this assumption, he stated the equality: total profit = investments + capitalists' consumption, as early as in his *Essays in the Theory of Economic Fluctuations*, London, 1938, p. 76. He resumed the same equality in a later note ('A Theory of Profit', *The Economic Journal*, 1942), where he explicitly stressed the one-way (causal) process through which profits are determined. 'It is . . . their [i.e. the capitalists'] investment and consumption decisions which determine profits, and not the other way round' (p. 259).

It is interesting that the procedure of recasting Keynesian theories in terms of simultaneous equations has also been attempted with reference to the theory of income distribution. In a Ph.D. thesis submitted at the London School of Economics in 1950 and published only recently (F. H. Hahn, *The Share of Wages*, London, 1972, but see also his 'The Share of Wages into National Income', *Oxford Economic Papers*, 1951, pp. 147–57), the author postulates two different relations between the share of wages (or the share of profits) and output: one is Kalecki's relation, according to which output and share of profit are inversely related; and the other is a newly proposed equation, based on entrepreneurs' utilities, according to which the supply of output and the share of profits are positively related. Hahn then claims that these two relations – in a demand and supply fashion – simultaneously determine output and income distribution.

This procedure – if my interpretation is correct – goes against both Keynes' and Kalecki's most fruitful and very basic idea of a one-way direction process through which investments determine savings. It was precisely by extending this process to the long-run, and by taking full-employment investments as an independent variable, that Kaldor has been able (given differentiated saving propensities) to turn the investments-savings determining process into a long-run theory of income distribution.

Assumption $n > 0$ (a positive rate of growth of the labour force) leaves all the results of the previous section unchanged, except that, on the equilibrium growth path, total wages increase at the natural rate of growth $g_n = n + \lambda$, while the wage-rate increases at the rate of growth of productivity $\lambda$. (Total growth of wages is accounted for partly by a widening of the labour force and partly by a growth of wages per man.)

A positive propensity to save of the workers leads Kaldor to work out two expressions for the profit share and for the rate of profit which are more complicated than (IV.15) and (IV.16). He remarks that $(S/Y) = s_w \, W/Y + s_c \, P/Y$, and since, in equilibrium, $(S/Y) = I/Y$, he substitutes into (IV.14) and arrives at[24]:

$$\frac{P}{Y} = \frac{1}{s_c - s_w} \frac{I}{Y} - \frac{s_w}{s_c - s_w}, \qquad (\text{IV.17})$$

$$\frac{P}{K} = \frac{1}{s_c - s_w} \frac{I}{K} - \frac{s_w}{s_c - s_w} \frac{Y}{K}. \qquad (\text{IV.18})$$

These expressions reduce to (IV.15) and (IV.16), respectively, in the particular case in which $s_w = 0$.

But most of all, Kaldor introduces further specific assumptions on the behaviour of the economic system, in order to be able to give an interpretation of how a capitalist economy actually behaves. His view is that capitalist systems normally go through two phases.[25] In an early phase, the capital stock is insufficient to provide employment for the whole existing labour force, so that there is unemployment of the Marxian type (a 'reserve army of labour'). The wage-rate is kept down to subsistence level and the capitalists can accumulate whatever savings they are able to make. In terms of the Harrod–Domar equation, the saving ratio becomes the bottleneck and the rate of growth (by becoming detached from population growth) becomes the variable.

But as soon as the whole 'reserve army of labour' is absorbed into employment, the system comes to a second phase, which is the one that has been considered in the previous section. The natural rate of growth $g_n$ becomes the bottleneck and the saving ratio $s$ becomes the variable. And since the aggregate saving ratio cannot go beyond $\kappa \, g_n$, the wage-rate must increase at the same rate of growth as productivity,

[24] These formulae will be discussed and criticized in Essay v.

[25] See especially: N. Kaldor, 'Capital Accumulation and Economic Growth', in *The Theory of Capital, Proceedings of a Conference held by the I.E.A.* ed. by F. A. Lutz and D. C. Hague, London, 1961, pp. 177–222.

if full employment is to be preserved. The specific assumptions that Kaldor uses here – investment being taken as an independent variable governed by population growth and technical progress – is that prices are more flexible than wages to changes of demand, at least within certain limits[26]; in other words, that profit margins are flexible in response to fluctuations of demand. If this is so, the share of profit and the rate of profit represented by the above expressions will not only be the *equilibrium* ones but actually those that tend to be realized in the long run.[27]

It is important to underline, as in the case of Harrod, that Kaldor's hypotheses on the actual behaviour of an economic system are not essential to expressions (IV.17) and (IV.18), or for that matter to (IV.15) and (IV.16). As conditions for long-run equilibrium, these expressions are valid in any case, whether Kaldor's behavioural hypotheses stand or fall. (In other words, if full employment of the labour force and full capacity utilization are aims to be pursued, those relations represent what is to be brought about, whether through Kaldor's mechanism or through any other institutional mechanism.)

### 9. *Concluding remarks*

A comparison with Ricardo's analysis becomes extremely illuminating at this point. Although starting from the same theoretical framework, Kaldor arrives at diametrically opposite conclusions. The reversal of Malthus' view on the relative growth of production and population, and the requirements of full-employment effective demand lead to a turning upside down of Ricardo's answer to the problem of income distribution. For Ricardo the wage-rate is fixed exogenously and all that remains (after paying rents) goes to profits. For Kaldor the rate of profit is determined exogenously by the natural rate of growth and the

[26] Kaldor (as Ricardo) is convinced that there is a limit below which the rate of profit cannot fall – a limit below which enterpreneurs would refuse to carry out investments. Likewise he is convinced that there is a limit below which the *real* wage-rates cannot fall. For if they did, the Trade Unions would permanently press for higher wages and a spiralling inflation would set in. Kaldor's mechanism is meant to work when neither of these limits has been reached.

[27] Suppose that, starting from an initial equilibrium situation, the workers succeed, through Trade Union pressure, in obtaining a share of wages in national income which is higher than the equilibrium share. The consequence is that aggregate effective demand will be higher than productive capacity (for, investment being fixed *ex hypothesis*, consumption will be higher than equilibrium consumption). If prices respond quicker than wages, prices will increase, profit margins will widen, the profit share will increase and the wage share will be brought back to equilibrium level. The same mechanism will operate in the opposite direction, if capitalists try to obtain a share of profit higher than the equilibrium one.

capitalists' propensity to save; and all that remains goes to wages. For the former it is profits that take up the features of a residual category; for the latter it is wages. It follows, for example, to take a problem of concern to both, that for Ricardo all taxes eventually fall on profits, while for Kaldor all taxes eventually fall on wages.[28]

But the most striking contrast of all lies in the basically more optimistic outlook that emerges on the evolution of capitalist systems. It has been argued after the publication of the *General Theory* that Keynes, by pointing out the necessity of keeping up effective demand and by suggesting a recipe for doing so, has contributed to salvaging the capitalist system from collapse.[29] But a full assessment of all the implications of full employment still remains to be made. The foregoing analysis takes us a step further. It shows that the necessity of maintaining full employment keeps savings to being no more than a certain proportion of national income, which in turn requires – if a constant fraction of profits is saved – that the wage-rate rises *pari passu* with productivity. The worst of Malthus' and Ricardo's fears, and the most frightening of Marx's predictions (that real wage-rates would be nailed down to subsistence and all surplus above subsistence would be appropriated by the capitalists) thereby turn out to be incompatible with the maintainance of full employment. In terms of exploitation, one may say that exploitation is indeed possible but only partially – to the extent allowed by capitalists' consumption and accumulation. Once these are provided for, full employment can be maintained only if the whole increasing productivity goes to wages.

And yet there is very little ground for complacency, even if the outlook is no longer so bleak as it used to be among the Classical representatives of 'the dismal science'. If the so much feared increasing immiserization of the working class is avoided, and a continually growing level of per-capita wages takes place instead, one can hardly attribute it to any intrinsic merit of a capitalist system. What is taking place is imposed by the requirements of survival. The system could not last otherwise – it would be doomed to slump and collapse.

---

[28] Both Ricardo and Kaldor have argued their views on taxation rather forcibly. (D. Ricardo, *On the Principles of Political Economy and Taxation;* N. Kaldor, *An Expenditure Tax*, London, 1955.)

[29] See, for example, J. K. Galbraith, *American Capitalism—The Concept of Countervailing Power*, Boston, Mass., 1952, especially chapter vi.

# V

# Rate of profit and income distribution in relation to the rate of economic growth*

One of the most exciting results of the macro-economic theories which have been elaborated in Cambridge is a very simple relation connecting the rate of profit and the distribution of income to the rate of economic growth, through the inter-action of the different propensities to save. The interesting aspect of this relation is that – by utilizing the Keynesian concepts of income determination by effective demand and of investment as a variable independent of consumption and savings – it gives a neat and modern content to the deep-rooted old Classical idea of a certain connection between distribution of income and capital accumulation. In this sense, it represents a break with the hundred-year-old tradition of marginal economic theory, and it is no wonder that it has immediately become the target of attacks and eulogies of such strongly emotional character. Approval and rejection have almost invariably co-incided with the commentators' marginalistic or non-marginalistic view.

The purpose of this essay is to present a more logical reconsideration of the whole theoretical framework, regarded as a system of necessary relations to achieve full employment. A proof will be given that the model, as originally formulated, cannot be maintained. However, once the necessary modifications are introduced, the conclusions which emerge appear much more general and – it seems to me – much more interesting than the authors themselves thought them to be.

## 1. *A post-Keynesian theory of income distribution and of the rate of profit*

The profit and distribution theory which is common to a number of macro-dynamic models elaborated in Cambridge has emerged as a

* Originally published in *The Review of Economic Studies*, vol. XXIX, no. 4, October 1962, pp. 267–79.

development of the Harrod–Domar model of economic growth.[1] As is well-known, all these models are theories of *long-run equilibrium*. They consider full employment systems where the possibilities of economic growth are externally given by population increase and technical progress. Therefore, the amount of investment – in physical terms – necessary in order to keep full employment through time, is also externally given. The interesting device which has made the analytical formulation of these models so simple and manageable consists in assuming that the externally given possibilities of growth increase at a *steady proportional rate* through time, i.e., according to an exponential function. When this happens, and the corresponding investments are actually carried out, all economic quantities grow in time at the same proportional rate of growth, so that all the ratios among them (investment to income, savings to income, rate of profit, etc.) remain constant. The system expands though keeping proportions constant.

Now, for any given rate of population growth and of (neutral) technical progress – i.e. for any given *natural rate of growth*, in Harrod's terminology – there is only one saving ratio which keeps the system in equilibrium growth. This sounds an awkwardly rigid conclusion. But the Cambridge economists have gone on to show that an externally given *aggregate* saving ratio is not incompatible with independently given individual propensities to save, because the aggregate ratio is simply a weighted average of individual ratios, where the weights represent individual shares in national income. Therefore, within certain limits, there always is a distribution of income at which the system produces the required amount of savings.

On this problem it is useful to follow the neat and simple formulation given by Mr Kaldor [which has been presented already, in detail, in

---

[1] The theory of distribution is due to Nicholas Kaldor. [See Essay iv above.] The relation of the rate of profit to the rate of growth has a longer history. In the thirties, J. von Neumann and also N. Kaldor, while still accepting a marginal productivity theory of the rate of profit, analysed the case of a slave economy, showing that the rate of growth is maximum when it is equal to the rate of profit. (J. von Neumann, 'A Model of General Economic Equilibrium', *The Review of Economic Studies* 1945–6, pp. 1–9, a paper first presented at a seminar of Princeton University in 1932; N. Kaldor, 'The Controversy on the Theory of Capital', *Econometrica*, 1937, pp. 228 ff.). It was, however, only with the recent macro-dynamic models that the causal link has been reversed. A relation of *dependence* of the rate of profit on the rate of growth appeared first, in the form of verbal statements supplemented with an arithmetical example, in Joan Robinson, *The Accumulation of Capital*, London, 1956, p. 255, and then, in the shape of a formal equation, in Nicholas Kaldor, 'A Model of Economic Growth', *The Economic Journal*, 1957, pp. 591–624. The same formal relation has been adopted by Richard Kahn, 'Exercises in the Analysis of Growth', *Oxford Economic Papers*, 1959, pp. 143–56.

sections 7–8 of Essay IV above]. Consider total net income ($Y$) as divided into two broad categories, wages and profits ($W$ and $P$); and total net savings as also divided into two categories, workers' savings ($S_w$) and capitalists' savings ($S_c$), so that:

$$Y \equiv W + P, \tag{v.1}$$

$$S \equiv S_w + S_c. \tag{v.2}$$

Suppose now simple proportional savings functions $S_w = s_w W$ and $S_c = s_c P$ (where $s_w$ and $s_c$, both being no less than zero and no more than unity, and $s_w \neq s_c$, represent the propensities to save of the workers and of the capitalists respectively). Suppose, moreover, that the amount of investment necessary to cope with population growth and technical progress – which we may call $I$ – is actually carried out. (This assumption is taken to mean that in the long run – provided that the rate of profit stays above a certain minimum level, below which capitalists would refuse to invest – decisions concerning investment are governed by the possibilities of expansion of the markets.) The condition under which the system will remain in a dynamic equilibrium, namely:

$$I = S, \tag{v.3}$$

has straightforward implications. Substituting from the saving functions:

$$I = s_w W + s_c P = s_w Y + (s_c - s_w)P,$$

whence:

$$\frac{P}{Y} = \frac{1}{s_c - s_w} \frac{I}{Y} - \frac{s_w}{s_c - s_w}, \tag{v.4}$$

and

$$\frac{P}{K} = \frac{1}{s_c - s_w} \frac{I}{K} - \frac{s_w}{s_c - s_w} \frac{Y}{K}, \tag{v.5}$$

which means that there is a distribution of income between wages and profits – equation (v.4) – and a corresponding rate of profit – equation (v.5) – at which the equilibrium condition (v.3) remains satisfied through time. Two particular cases of special interest arise when $s_w = 0$, so that (v.4) and (v.5) become:

$$\frac{P}{Y} = \frac{1}{s_c} \frac{I}{Y}, \quad \text{and} \quad \frac{P}{K} = \frac{1}{s_c} \frac{I}{K};$$

and when $s_c = 1$ (besides $s_w = 0$) in which case, (v.4) and (v.5) simply reduce to:

$$\frac{P}{Y} = \frac{I}{Y}, \quad \text{and} \quad \frac{P}{K} = \frac{I}{K}.$$

It is the two more general equations (v.4) and (v.5) which have been considered so far as expressing what we may call the post-Keynesian theory of income distribution and of the rate of profit. To them we must add two restrictions, in order to limit the validity of the mathematical formulations to the range in which they have an economic meaning; namely:

$$s_w < \frac{I}{Y},$$ (v.6)

and

$$s_c > \frac{I}{Y}.$$ (v.7)

Restriction (v.6) excludes the case of a dynamic equilibrium with a null or negative share of profit, and restriction (v.7) excludes the case of a dynamic equilibrium with a null or negative share of wages. In practice, if (v.6) were not satisfied, the system would enter a situation of chronic Keynesian underemployment. Similarly, if (v.7) were not satisfied, the system would enter a situation of chronic inflation. (As a matter of fact the latter limit becomes operative much before $s_c$ ever approaches $I/Y$, because there is a minimum level below which the wage-rate cannot be compressed.) It is within these limits that the above model is meant to apply, and that equations (v.4) and (v.5) show the existence of a distribution of income and a rate of profit which, through time, will keep the system in equilibrium.

Mr Kaldor has gone further. He has pointed out that, if there is in the system a price mechanism by which the level of prices with respect to the money wages (i.e. profit margins) is determined by demand; and if $s_c > s_w$ – which after all is implied by (v.6)–(v.7) – then income distribution (v.4) and rate of profit (v.5) will not only exist but also will be the ones that the system actually tends to produce.

## 2. *A correction*

There is a logical slip, in the theory reported above, which has so far passed unnoticed. The authors have neglected the important fact that, in any type of society, when any individual saves a part of his income, he must also be allowed to own it, otherwise he would not save at all. This means that the stock of capital which exists in the system is owned by those people (capitalists or workers) who in the past made the corresponding savings. And since ownership of capital entitles the owner to a rate of interest, if workers have saved – and thus own a part of the stock of capital (directly or through loans to the capitalists) – then they will also receive a share of the total profits. Therefore total profits themselves must be divided into two categories: profits which accrue to the capitalists and profits which accrue to the workers.

It is this distinction that is missing in the theory just considered. By attributing all profits to the capitalists it has inadvertently but necessarily implied that workers' savings are always totally transferred as a gift to the capitalists. Clearly this is an absurdity. To eliminate it, we must reformulate the model from the beginning and clear up the confusion which has been made of two different concepts of distribution of income: distribution of income between profits and wages, and distribution of income between capitalists and workers. The two concepts only coincide in the particular case in which there is no saving out of wages.

### 3. *Reformulating the model*

For a correct reformulation of the model, we must resume equations (v.1)–(v.3) and add a further identity:

$$P \equiv P_c + P_w ,$$

where $P_c$ and $P_w$ stand for profits which accrue to the capitalists and profits which accrue to the workers. The saving functions now become $S_w = s_w(W + P_w)$ and $S_c = s_c P_c$; and the equilibrium condition becomes:

$$I = s_w(W + P_w) + s_c P_c = s_w Y + (s_c - s_w)P_c ,$$

from which – by following exactly the same steps which led to equations (v.4) and (v.5) – we obtain:

$$\frac{P_c}{Y} = \frac{1}{s_c - s_w} \frac{I}{Y} - \frac{s_w}{s_c - s_w} , \tag{v.8}$$

and

$$\frac{P_c}{K} = \frac{1}{s_c - s_w} \frac{I}{K} - \frac{s_w}{s_c - s_w} \frac{Y}{K} . \tag{v.9}$$

As the reader can see, the right-hand sides of (v.8) and (v.9) exactly coincide with the right-hand sides of (v.4) and (v.5), but the left-hand sides do not. This means that the expressions used so far *do not refer to total profits*. They only refer to that part of profits which accrue to the capitalists. Let us examine the implications.

As far as the distribution theory is concerned, equation (v.8) still retains a definite, but restricted, meaning. It now only expresses the distribution of income between capitalists and workers. The distribution of income between profits and wages is something different, and to obtain it, one must add the share of workers' profit into income ($P_w/Y$) to both sides of equation (v.8). As to the theory of the rate of profit, the consequences of our reformulation are even more serious. Expression (v.9) simply represents the ratio of a *part* of profits ($P_c$) to *total* capital, but this concept has no useful or interesting meaning. The expression which is really needed is one for the ratio of total profits to total capital (rate of profit), and to obtain it, we must again add a ratio ($P_w/K$) to both sides of equation (v.9). In other words, we have to find suitable expressions for:

$$\frac{P}{Y} = \frac{P_c}{Y} + \frac{P_w}{Y}, \tag{v.10}$$

and

$$\frac{P}{K} = \frac{P_c}{K} + \frac{P_w}{K}.$$

Let us start with the latter equation. We know $P_c/K$ already from (v.9). Thus, writing $K_w$ for the amount of capital that the workers own indirectly – through loans to the capitalists – and $i$ for the rate of interest on these loans, we obtain:

$$\frac{P}{K} = \frac{1}{s_c - s_w} \frac{I}{K} - \frac{s_w}{s_c - s_w} \frac{Y}{K} + \frac{iK_w}{K}.$$

An expression for $K_w/K$ can easily be found. In dynamic equilibrium:

$$\frac{K_w}{K} = \frac{S_w}{S} = \frac{s_w(Y - P_c)}{I} = \frac{s_w s_c}{s_c - s_w} \frac{Y}{I} - \frac{s_w}{s_c - s_w},$$

which, after substitution into the previous expression, finally gives us:

$$\frac{P}{K} = \frac{1}{s_c - s_w} \frac{I}{K} - \frac{s_w}{s_c - s_w} \frac{Y}{K} + i\left(\frac{s_w s_c}{s_c - s_w} \frac{Y}{I} - \frac{s_w}{s_c - s_w}\right). \tag{v.11}$$

By exactly following the same procedure, the expression for equation (v.10) comes out as:

$$\frac{P}{Y} = \frac{1}{s_c - s_w} \frac{I}{Y} - \frac{s_w}{s_c - s_w} + i\left(\frac{s_w s_c}{s_c - s_w} \frac{K}{I} - \frac{s_w}{s_c - s_w} \frac{K}{Y}\right). \tag{v.12}$$

These are the two general equations we were looking for. By now, we have all the elements which are necessary to correct the post-Keynesian theory of income distribution and of the rate of profit. Equation (v.5) of section 1, expressing the rate of profit, must be replaced by equation (v.11); and equation (v.4) must be replaced by two distinct equations: equation (v.8) for the distribution of income between workers and capitalists, and equation (v.12) for the distribution of income between wages and profits.

### 4. *Rate and share of profits in relation to the rate of growth*

The most immediate consequence of the reformulation which has just been carried out is that, in order to say anything about share and rate of profits, one needs first a *theory of the rate of interest*. In a long-run equilibrium model, the obvious hypothesis to make is that of a rate of interest equal to the rate of profit. If we do make such a hypothesis, equations (v.11) and (v.12) become very simple indeed. By substituting $P/K$ for $i$, in equation (v.11), we get:

$$\frac{P}{K}\left(1 - \frac{s_w s_c}{s_c - s_w} \cdot \frac{Y}{I} + \frac{s_w}{s_c - s_w}\right) = \frac{1}{s_c - s_w} \frac{I}{K} - \frac{s_w}{s_c - s_w} \frac{Y}{K},$$

$$\frac{P}{K} \frac{s_c(I - s_w Y)}{I} = \frac{I - s_w Y}{K}.$$

Whence, provided that:

$$I - s_w Y \neq 0, \tag{v.13}$$

(otherwise the ratio $P/K$ would be indeterminate) the whole expression simply becomes:

$$\frac{P}{K} = \frac{1}{s_c} \frac{I}{K}. \tag{v.14}$$

And by an analogous process, equation (v.12) reduces to:

$$\frac{P}{Y} = \frac{1}{s_c} \frac{I}{Y}. \tag{v.15}$$

The reader will notice that these results are formally similar to those which have been shown in section 1 as particular cases. But now they have been reached without making any assumption whatsoever on the propensities to save of the workers. This is the most striking result of our analysis. It means that, in the long run, workers' propensity to save, though influencing the distribution of income between capitalists and workers – equation (v.8) – does not influence the distribution of income between profits and wages – equation (v.15). Nor does it have any influence whatsoever on the rate of profit – equation (v.14)!

### 5. *A fundamental relation between profits and savings*

The novelty of the conclusion reached in the previous section makes it perhaps worth while trying to investigate a little more closely the logic behind it.

Let me point out immediately that the model has been built on the institutional principle, inherent in any production system, that wages are distributed among the members of society in proportion to the amount of labour they contribute and profits are distributed in proportion to the amount of capital they own. The latter proposition implies something which has passed unnoticed so far, namely that, in the long run, profits will turn out to be distributed in proportion to the amount of savings which are contributed. In other words, no matter how many categories of individuals we may consider, in a long-run exponential growth, the ratio of the profits that each category receives to the savings that it provides will always be the same for all categories. In our model:

$$\frac{P_w}{S_w} = \frac{P_c}{S_c}.$$ (v.16)

This indeed sets a proportionality relation between profits and savings which is fundamental to the whole problem of profits and distribution. It means that, for each category, *profits are in the long run proportional to savings*. Let me stress that this relation does not depend on any behavioural assumption whatsoever; it simply and logically follows from the institutional principle that profits are distributed in proportion to ownership of capital.

This principle, however, still leaves the actual value of ratio (v.16) indeterminate, as it only requires that this ratio be the same for all categories. It is at this point that the particular types of income out of which savings are made become relevant. If there is in the system a category of individuals who – owing to the position they occupy in the production process – derive all their incomes, and therefore savings, exclusively from profits, the saving behaviour of just this group of individuals will set up, independently of (v.16), another and more definite relation between savings and profits. The only way in which this new behavioural relation can be compatible with (v.16) is for it to determine the actual value of the ratio of profits to savings for the whole system. We can see this immediately by substituting our saving functions into (v.16). We obtain:

$$\frac{P_w}{s_w(W + P_w)} = \frac{P_c}{s_c P_c},$$

which may also be written in either of the two following ways:

$$s_w(W + P_w) = s_c P_w \ , \qquad\qquad (v.17)$$

or

$$s_w W = [(1 - s_w) - (1 - s_c)]P_w \ . \qquad\qquad (v.18)$$

These expressions now allow us some insight into the reason why workers' propensity to save does not, and capitalists' propensity to save does, play a role in determining *total* profits. Expression (v.17) says that, in the long run, when workers save, they receive an amount of profits $(P_w)$ such as to make their total savings exactly equal to the amount that the capitalists would have saved out of workers' profits $(P_w)$ if these profits remained to them. Expression (v.18) is even more explicit. Savings out of wages always turn out to be equal to workers' extra consumption out of profits (extra consumption meaning consumption in excess of what the capitalists would have consumed if those profits remained to them). Another way of interpreting these results is to say that whatever workers' propensity to save $(s_w)$ may be, there is always a distribution of income and a distribution of profits which makes the ratio $P_w/s_w(W + P_w)$ equal to any pre-determined ratio $P_w/S_w$. Or, to look at the problem the other way round, for any given $s_w$, there are infinite proportions between profits and savings which can be used in (v.16) and which at the same time can make $P_w/s_w(W + P_w)$ equal to $P_w/S_w$. All this is, after all, a complicated way of saying that, on the part of the workers, the rate of profit is indeterminate. They will always receive, in the long run, an amount of profits proportional to their savings, whatever the rate of profit may be.

The situation is entirely different when we consider the capitalists. The fact that all capitalists' savings come out of profits sets a straight relation between savings and profits. No other variable enters into it, in contrast with the previous case where the wage share was also in the picture. It follows that, for any given $s_c$, there is only one proportionality relation between profits and savings – this relation being required by (v.16) – which can also make the ratio $P_c/s_c P_c$ equal to $P_c/S_c$. This proportionality relation can be nothing but $s_c$, which will therefore determine the ratio of profits to savings for all the saving groups, and consequently also the income distribution between profits and wages and the rate of profit for the whole system. The reader may complete his view of the problem by thinking for a moment of the practically irrelevant but interesting case, in which capitalists' profits are nil (i.e. $P_c = 0$). In this case, the behavioural relation $(s_c P_c)$ determining the rate of profit drops out of the picture altogether and the rate of profit becomes indeterminate. (The parameter $s_w$, which remains, cannot determine the rate of profit!) We have met this case already in the process of finding $P/K$, in section 4, where non-fulfilment of (v.13) would exactly imply $P_c = 0$ and an indeterminate rate of profit.

## 6. *Implications*

We may now synthesize the implications of the foregoing analysis in two conclusions. First of all, the irrelevance of workers' propensity to save gives the model a much wider generality than was hitherto believed. Since the rate of profit and the income distribution between profits and wages are determined independently of $s_w$, there is no need for any hypothesis whatever on the *aggregate* savings behaviour of the workers. The non-capitalists might well be divided into any number of sub-categories one likes; the subdivision might even be carried as far as to consider single individuals; yet equations (v.14)–(v.15) would not change. Of course the particular behaviour of the sub-categories or single individuals would influence the distribution of income among the various workers, and between the workers and the capitalists, as equation (v.8) shows. But the distribution of income between total wages and total profits, and the rate of profit would remain exactly the same.

Secondly, the relevance of the capitalists' propensity to save, which is the only one to appear in the final formulae (v.14) and (v.15), uncovers the absolutely strategic importance for the whole system of the decisions to save of just one group of individuals: the capitalists. The particular saving function of this group transforms the open proportionality relation (v.16) into a definite function in which the proportion that profits must bear to savings *in the whole system*, is given by the saving propensity of one single category of individuals[2]. The similar decisions to save of all the other individuals, the workers, do not count in this

---

[2] It may be useful to remind the reader that the whole analysis refers to states of long-run equilibrium. The relevant behavioural process must not necessarily be looked for in association with particular physical persons, but rather in association with specific kinds of decisions: those concerning savings out of profits as such. It must, moreover, be noticed that in a modern economic system, where large corporations have a certain autonomous power to retain profits, the profit retention ratios of the corporations and the individuals' propensities to save out of (distributed) profits add up.

respect. Whatever the workers may do, they can only share in an amount of total profits which for them is predetermined; they have no power to influence it at all.

These conclusions, as the reader may clearly realise, now suddenly shed new light on the old Classical idea, hinted at already at the beginning, of a relation between the savings of that group of individuals who are in the position to carry on the process of production and the process of capital accumulation. This idea has always persisted in economic literature but in a vague and muddled form. Economists have never been able to bring it out clearly. In particular they have always thought – and the post-Keynesian theories examined in section 1 seemed to confirm – that the relation between capitalists' savings and capital accumulation depended on particularly simplifying and drastic assumptions about negligible savings by the workers. The novelty of the present analysis has been to show that the relation is valid independently of any of those assumptions. It is valid whatever the saving behaviour of the workers may be.

## 7. *The conditions of stability*

Our analysis would be incomplete if, after showing that there exists a distribution of income between profits and wages which keeps the system in long-run equilibrium, we did not also specify the limits within which such distribution has economic meaning and the conditions under which it is stable.

On this problem we may recall the discussion that Mr Kaldor has already carried out. The limits (v.6) and (v.7) of section 1 must here be confirmed. Moreover, we must confirm that if there is in the system a price mechanism by which the level of prices with respect to the level of wages (profit margins) rises or falls according as to whether demand exceeds or falls short of supply, and if equilibrium investments are actually carried out, then the system is stable. For it will tend to get back to its dynamic equilibrium path whenever displaced from it.

But we are now in a position to examine these problems in a much better way. The propositions stated above may be expressed as follows:

$$\frac{\mathrm{d}}{\mathrm{d}t}\left(\frac{P}{Y}\right) = f\left(\frac{I}{Y} - \frac{S}{Y}\right), \qquad \text{(v.19)}$$

with the properties:

$$f(0) = 0,$$
$$f' > 0,$$

113

which simply means that, as time ($t$) goes on, the profit margins, and therefore the share of total profits, remain constant, increase or decrease according as to whether total savings produced by the system tend to be equal, smaller, or greater than total investments.

Equation (v.19) is a simple differential equation. By solving it with respect to deviations from the equilibrium share of profits,[3] the only requirement for stability emerges as:

$$\frac{d(I/Y)}{d(P/Y)} < \frac{d(S/Y)}{d(P/Y)}, \qquad (v.20)$$

which means that the response of $I/Y$ to deviations of $P/Y$ from its equilibrium value must be smaller than the response of $S/Y$. But, in our model, there can be no response of $I/Y$ to $P/Y$ because $I$ has been defined as that amount of investments which has to be undertaken in order to keep full employment over time. This amount of investments, as a proportion of total income, is uniquely determined from outside the economic system, by technology and population growth[4]; and the

---

[3] Call $(P/Y)^*$ the equilibrium value of $P/Y$ at which $(I/Y) - (S/Y) = 0$. By expanding (v.19) in Taylor series around this equilibrium value, and neglecting the terms of higher order than the first, we obtain:

$$\frac{d}{dt}\left[\frac{P}{Y} - \left(\frac{P}{Y}\right)^*\right] = f(0) + f'(0)\left[\frac{d(I/Y)}{d(P/Y)} - \frac{d(S/Y)}{d(P/(Y))}\right]_{(P/Y)^*}\left[\frac{P}{Y} - \left(\frac{P}{Y}\right)^*\right],$$

where the last but one square brackets contain derivatives taken at the particular point $(P/Y)^*$, so that the whole term is constant. Calling now:

$$\left[\frac{d(I/Y)}{d(P/Y)} - \frac{d(S/Y)}{d(P/Y)}\right]_{(P/Y)^*} = m,$$

and integrating, we obtain:

$$\left[\frac{P}{Y} - \left(\frac{P}{Y}\right)^*\right]_t = \left[\frac{P}{Y} - \left(\frac{P}{Y}\right)^*\right]_0 e^{f'mt}.$$

Since $f' > 0$, the only condition for this expression to tend to zero as time goes on (i.e. for the system to be stable) is $m < 0$.

[4] Those readers who have been brought up in the neo-classical tradition might think that I am implicitly assuming the existence of only one technique of production. Since I am not, it may be useful to clarify the issue by making explicit the implications of the foregoing analysis for what has been called the *neo-classical* theory of economic growth (as expounded, for example, by Professor Solow in a 'Contribution to the Theory of Economic Growth', *The Quarterly Journal of Economics*, 1956, or by Professor Meade in *A Neo-Classical Theory of Economic Growth*, London, 1961). Suppose there exists an infinite number of possible techniques expressed by a traditional production function:

$$Y = F(K, L), \qquad (1')$$

share of profits can in no way alter it. Therefore:

$$\frac{d(I/Y)}{d(P/Y)} = 0.$$

We are thus left with the right-hand side of (v.20) required to be greater than zero. After substituting from the savings functions:

$$\frac{d(S/Y)}{d(P/Y)} = \frac{d}{d(P/Y)}\left(s_w \frac{W}{Y} + s_w \frac{P_w}{Y} + s_c \frac{P - P_w}{Y}\right) > 0. \quad \text{(v.21)}$$

---

assumed to be homogenous of the first degree and invariant to time; and suppose that labour $(L)$ is increasing at an externally given rate of growth $n$, so that $L(t) = L(0)e^{nt}$. The whole previous analysis remains unaltered. We may now read $F(K,L)$ whenever we have written $Y$, and we may write, if we like, the final expression (v.14) as:

$$s_c[F(K, L) - W] = I. \tag{2'}$$

However, as we have assumed more information about technology, we can now inquire further into the composition of investments. By defining $k = K/L$, so that $K = kL$, we may write investment as:

$$\frac{dK}{dt} = k\,\frac{dL}{dt} + L\,\frac{dk}{dt} = knL + L\,\frac{dk}{dt}.$$

But on the steady growth path $(dk/dt) = 0$, so that $I = knL$. And substituting into (2') the equilibrium relation becomes:

$$s_c[F(K, L) - W] = \frac{K}{L} nL,$$

whence:

$$\frac{P}{K} = \frac{n}{s_c}. \tag{3'}$$

The equilibrium rate of profit is determined by the natural rate of growth divided by the capitalists' propensity to save; independently of anything else in the model. This basic relation is confirmed. Therefore, the link between (v.14) and (v.15) that the extra technical equation (1') has introduced, can only go one way. Since it cannot influence the rate of profit, it can only contribute to determining the investment–income ratio. In this way the equilibrium amount of investment is uniquely and exogenously determined. All this means that the foregoing analysis has singled out one of those asymmetrical chains of relations to which in science the concept of causality is associated. This causality chain may here be expressed as follows. The externally given rate of population growth and the capitalists' propensity to save determine first of all the rate of profit. At this rate of profit, the optimum technique is chosen (in such a way as to satisfy the marginal productivity conditions). Then, the optimum technique, together with the rate of population growth, uniquely determine the equilibrium investment–income ratio. In this system, therefore, technical relation (1') simply comes to determine one more variable – the equilibrium amount of capital.

We may first consider an intermediate step. In the short run, the share of profits which accrue to the workers is fixed, as it takes time for the rate of interest to adapt itself to the rate of profit (even if the two coincide in the long run). And since:

$$\frac{\mathrm{d}(W/Y)}{\mathrm{d}(P/Y)} = -1,$$

condition (v.21) becomes:

$$s_c - s_w > 0.$$

This is exactly the stability condition given by Mr Kaldor. The above analysis proves that it is only a short-run condition.

But let us consider the long run, when the share of workers' profits is no longer fixed and $P_w$ adapts itself to a proportion of $K_w$ equal to the proportion that $P_c$ bears to $K_c$. By substitution from (v.18), condition (v.21) simply becomes:

$$s_c > 0.$$

This is all that is required. We may conclude that, in a system where full employment investments are actually carried out, and prices are flexible with respect to wages, the only condition for stability is $s_c > 0$, a condition which is certainly and abundantly satisfied even outside the limits in which the mathematical model has an economic meaning.

## 8. *The case of a socialist system*

Going back now to our basic model, the reader will notice how few, after all, are the assumptions which have been used. These assumptions become even fewer if we consider the case of a socialist system.

In a socialist society, all the members of the community belong to the category of workers. There is no place for capitalists; the responsibility for carrying on the production process and the direct ownership of all means of production are taken over by the State. However, the State, as such, cannot consume: consumption can be carried out only by individuals. Therefore, if any amount of the national product is not distributed to the members of the community, either as wages or as interest on their loans to the State, that amount is *ipso facto* saved. This means that the parameter $s_c$ becomes unity ($s_c = 1$), as an inherent property of the system; so that even the one behavioural parameter that still remained, in our final formulae, disappears.

Equations (v.14) and (v.15) become:

$$\frac{P}{Y} = \frac{I}{Y},$$ (v.22)

and

$$\frac{P}{K} = \frac{I}{K},$$ (v.23)

with the evident meaning that, in equilibrium, total profits are equal to total investments, and the rate of profit (and of interest) is equal to the ratio of investment to capital, i.e. equal to the *natural* rate of growth. It follows that total wages always turn out to be equal to total consumption and total profits always turn out to be equal to total savings. However, this does not mean that all wages are consumed and all profits are saved! The (v.22)–(v.23) have been reached without any assumption whatsoever on individual decisions to save. Each individual may be left completely free to decide the proportion of his income (wages plus interest) that he likes to save, without in the least affecting the (v.22)–(v.23). This result is simply the counterpart, for a socialist system, of what has been pointed out in section 4 as the most striking outcome of our analysis.

An explanation can be given by following the same procedure used in section 5, which here becomes even simpler. By putting $s_c = 1$ in (v.18), the interesting property immediately emerges that, in a dynamic equilibrium, individual savings out of wages are exactly equal to individual consumption out of interest; so that total consumption (out of wages and out of interest) turns out to be equal to total wages.

The important corollary that follows is that there is no need for a socialist State to exert any interference whatsoever in individual decisions to consume and to save. Only one limit must be respected, a limit which is the same encountered in the case of a capitalist system and is expressed by inequality (v.6). The community, as a whole, cannot remain in equilibrium if it insists in saving more than what is required by the *natural* rate of growth; if it did, the system would fall into a situation of chronic under-employment due to lack of effective demand.[5] Provided that this limit is not overcome, no restriction need be put on individual savings. The only effect of these savings is to require from the State the issuing of a national debt for a part of the stock of capital, and the consequent distribution of a part of profits, which will however come back under the form of lent savings.

[5] We are considering, of course, a closed system. In an open system, in which the State might lend abroad, full employment might be kept even if total savings go beyond required total investments.

To conclude, we may put these results in the following way. In a full employment economic system in which all net revenues that accrue to the organizers of the process of production are saved, there exists one particular rate of profit, which we may indeed call the *natural rate of profit* – since it turns out to be equal to the natural rate of growth – which has the following property. If it is applied both in the process of pricing and in the payment of interest on loans, it causes the system, *whatever the individual decisions to save may be*, to produce a total amount of savings which is exactly equal to the amount of investment needed to cope with technical progress and population growth.

## 9. *Models and reality*

At this point, the reader may have become a little impatient and may begin to wonder: but what is after all the practical relevance of the whole macro-economic exercise?

There are two different problems raised by this question. The first one concerns aggregation. It must be noticed that the foregoing investigation is not 'macro-economic' in the sense of representing a first simplified rough step towards a more detailed and disaggregated analysis. It is macro-economic because it could not be otherwise. Only problems have been discussed which are of a macro-economic nature; an accurate investigation of them has nothing to do with disaggregation. They would remain the same – i.e. they would still arise at a macro-economic level – even if we were to break down the model into a disaggregated analysis, and therefore introduce the necessary additional information (or assumptions) about consumers' choice of goods and producers' choice of techniques. I might add that, in fact, the present essay has originated from a *multi-sector* growth model, on which I have been working for some time,[6] and whose results have turned out to be incompatible with the post-Keynesian theories examined in section 1.

A second and separate problem concerns the interpretative value of the model. When Mr Kaldor presented his theory of income distribution, he pointed out that the interpretative value of the theory depends on the Keynesian hypotheses on which it is built. In particular it depends on the crucial hypothesis (post-Keynesian rather than Keynesian) that investment can be treated as an independent variable governed by technical progress and population growth.

[6] [Published as 'A New Theoretical Approach to the Problems of Economic Growth', *The Econometric Approach to Development Planning*, Pontificiae Academiae Scientiarum Scripta Varia no. 28, Vatican City, 1965, pp. 571–687.]

But this is not the approach that I should like to take here. Whether we are or whether we are not prepared to accept the model in this behavioural sense, there are important practical implications which are valid in any case. I should look, therefore, at the previous analysis simply and more generally as a logical framework to answer interesting questions about what *ought* to happen if full employment is to be kept over time, more than as a behavioural theory expressing what actually happens.

The case of a socialist system, which came last in our analysis, is the most straightforward on this respect. The amount of investment that must be undertaken in order to maintain full employment – once this has been reached – is indeed that which is required by technical progress and population growth. And if this investment is carried out, the rate of profit (when uniformly applied) must be equal to the natural rate of growth, if total demand is to be such as to allow the full utilization of the productive capacity and of the labour force. These results do not depend on any behavioural assumption whatsoever. They are true whatever individual behaviour may be; as a simple matter of logical necessity.

In the case of a capitalist system, the additional problem arises of whether the capitalists will or will not spontaneously undertake the amount of investment necessary to cope with the natural possibilities of growth. We may of course discuss at length in this case the circumstances under which equilibrium will or will not be automatically reached. But again we should not let these discussions obscure the conclusions, which are valid in any case, about the relations that must be satisfied if full employment is to be kept. If full employment is to be maintained, *that* amount of investment *must* be undertaken. And if it is undertaken; there is – for any given proportion of capitalists' income which tends to be saved[7] – only one rate of profit, i.e. one distribution of income between profits and wages, that keeps the system on the dynamic path of full employment.

This, it seems to me, is the relevant way to look at the model which has been elaborated above. The whole analysis has been carried out with constant reference to a situation of full employment because full

---

[7] Let me point out that, in this context, the objection so commonly advanced against the theory formulated in section 1 – namely, that to classify the members of a modern society in only two groups is an arbitrary and crude simplification – entirely loses its ground. The central outcome of the previous analysis precisely is that, as far as the determination of the rate of profit is concerned, the distinction between individuals who save exclusively out of profits and individuals who save out of wages is the only one that matters.

employment is the situation that matters, and that, indeed, now-a-days forms one of the agreed goals of any economic system. The conclusions, therefore, acquire an important practical relevance whether the system is automatically able to reach full employment or whether it is not. In the latter case, I should say that they become even more important, because it is then that practical measures have to be taken and it becomes essential to have clear ideas about the direction in which to move.

# VI

# The rate of profit in an expanding economy

The preceding essay has given rise to so many discussions, since its original publication, as to make it necessary for me to return to the subject. Enough time has now elapsed to render it possible to look at the results obtained in a sufficiently detached way.

Without attempting a complete review of the controversies that have taken place, which would take too long, I shall try to synthesize the contribution to knowledge which seems to me to have come from the discussions, and the generalizations it is now possible to make.*

## 1. Harrod–Domar's dilemma

The source of the discussions has remained the *impasse* which derives from the Harrod–Domar equilibrium relation:[1]

$$s = \kappa\, g_n, \qquad\qquad (\text{VI.1.1})$$

where: $s$ = savings to income ratio, $\kappa$ = capital–output ratio, $g_n$ = natural rate of growth. If these three magnitudes were all constant, then (VI.1.1) could only be satisfied by a fluke. This is what may be called the Harrod–Domar 'knife-edge' problem. Either the economic system happens to be on the particular 'knife-edge' equilibrium growth path defined by (VI.1.1), or no equilibrium growth is possible at all.

## 2. The 'Cambridge equation'

The obvious 'Keynesian' answer to the Harrod–Domar dilemma is the one proposed by Kaldor, and discussed in Essay IV. The aggregate savings to income ratio $s$, which we may well write as $S/Y$, cannot be considered as a constant, as it is a weighted average of the saving propensities of the various categories of savers. If, on Classical lines,

* In this essay, all references are listed at the end (pp. 145–6).
[1] See p. 96. (Essay IV).

we begin by considering two categories – workers and capitalists – with propensities to save $s_w$ and $s_c$, respectively, then:

$$g_n \, \kappa = \frac{S}{Y} = s_w \frac{W}{Y} + s_c \frac{P}{Y} , \qquad \text{(VI.2.1)}$$

where $W = $ total wages and $P = $ total profits; $W + P = Y$. The 'weights' in the weighted average are the shares of wages and of profits in the national income. Provided only that:

$$s_w < \kappa \, g_n < s_c , \qquad \text{(VI.2.2)}$$

there exists an equilibrium distribution of income between wages and profits which produces precisely that saving ratio that is required by equilibrium growth.

I argued in Essay v that there is a logical slip in this way of presenting the problem[2], but we can make this logical slip irrelevant, for the time being, by beginning with the Classical assumption that $s_w = 0$. In this case, we obtain immediately, from (VI.2.1),

$$\frac{P}{K} = \frac{1}{s_c} g_n , \qquad \text{(VI.2.3)}$$

where, of course, $(P/K) < Y/K$, to make economic sense.

Thus, within inequalities (VI.2.2), equilibrium growth is always possible, in spite of $\kappa, g_n, s_w, s_c$, all being constant. And the equilibrium rate of profit, as emerges from (VI.2.3), is determined by the natural rate of growth divided by the capitalists' propensity to save, independently of anything else. I shall call this relation, for short, the 'Cambridge equation'.

### 3. *The marginal productivity alternative*[3]

There has been an alternative answer to the Harrod–Domar 'knife-edge' problem, which it may be useful to consider straightaway. It has

[2] Samuelson and Modigliani [21, p. 270n] – though not Kaldor – have argued that such a 'logical slip' could be eliminated by interpreting Kaldor as assuming a certain propensity to save out of wages and a certain propensity to save out of profits (independently of whether profits are saved by workers or by capitalists). But this argument is erroneous. A workers' propensity to save out of profit equal to the capitalists' propensity to save is *incompatible with equilibrium growth*. For the rate of capital accumulation by the workers would be permanently higher than that of the capitalists. (See the arguments of section 7 below on capitalists' and workers' capital accumulation. See also Maneschi [6].)

[3] I am using the term 'marginal productivity', as it seems to me more appropriate than the term 'neoclassical', which has been generally used. The introduction of the notion of marginal productivity seems to be the only purpose of this approach, which has very little to do with Classical economics.

been proposed by the marginal productivity theorists[4], who have focused their attention on κ as the equilibrating variable. Their argument has been that net income $Y$ is a function (production function) of two 'factors of production', labour ($L$) and capital ($K$),

$$Y = f(L, K). \qquad (\text{vi.3.1})$$

This function is supposed to have positive first order partial derivatives (called 'marginal productivities') and negative second order partial derivatives (law of diminishing returns to changing proportions), and moreover to be homogeneous of the first degree so as to yield the following relation (Euler's theorem):

$$Y = \frac{\partial Y}{\partial K} K + \frac{\partial Y}{\partial L} L. \qquad (\text{vi.3.2})$$

Assuming perfect competition in both the labour market and the capital market, and assuming profit maximization behaviour, the wage-rate and the rate of profit will tend to the marginal productivities of labour and of capital respectively, while full employment will be assured by the choice of the appropriate proportion of capital to labour. This makes the capital–output ratio infinitely flexible and capable of varying from near zero to near infinity, as an inverse monotonic function of the rate of interest (which is supposed to be equal to the rate of profit). This function is shown in fig. vi.1, with κ on the ordinate and the rate of profit $r = P/K$ on the abscissa, both axes being the asymptotes of the function.

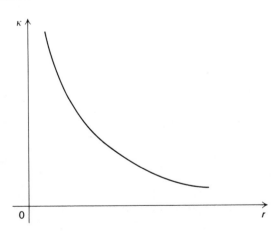

Fig. vi.1

4 Especially: Solow [24], Swan [26] and Meade [8].

The same scheme has then been adapted to the case in which there is technical progress, by assuming that function (VI.3.1) remains exactly the same through time but is shifted according to an exponential function in which, at the exponent, time multiplies the rate of growth of productivity.[5]

In this way, the capital–output ratio $\kappa$ is assumed to be squeezed into equality with the predetermined ratio $s/g_n$ by perfect competition, i.e.

$$\kappa = \frac{s}{g_n}. \tag{VI.3.3}$$

At this capital–output ratio, the marginal productivities of labour and of capital determine the wage-rate and the rate of profit respectively, while Euler's relation (VI.3.2) ensures the distribution of income between labour and capital without any residual whatever being left over.

The traditional theory of marginal productivity is thereby inserted into the Harrod–Domar model.[6]

## 4. *Extreme assumptions and general results*

I think I should state immediately why the marginal productivity approach appears to me not a generalization, but in fact a restriction of the Harrod–Domar analysis. There is, of course, nothing wrong with considering $\kappa$ as a variable. A discussion on this will be carried out in the following pages. But in marginal productivity analysis, though the stated purpose is always that of 'generalizing' the Harrod–Domar model from 'fixed' to 'flexible' proportions, a whole series of restrictive assumptions are in fact introduced.

Solow, for example, after writing that his work 'is devoted to a model of long-run growth which accepts all the Harrod–Domar assumptions except that of fixed proportions',[7] blithely goes on to add a whole

---

[5] This is what has been called 'Hicks neutral' technical progress, as opposed to the 'Harrod neutral' technical progress (see pp. 96–7), which, within the marginal productivity context, has been characterized by the same exponential function applied to *L* within the brackets in (VI.3.1), instead of being applied to the whole production function. Most marginal productivity analyses, however, use the particular 'Cobb–Douglas production function' for which the two types of neutral technical progress produce the same results.

[6] From a didactical point of view, the marginal productivity approach has had an enormous success. It has the advantage of building behind $\kappa$ a model which is sufficiently elegant and complicated as to command attention and respect; and of using concepts with which students of economics have been familiar for more than a century (especially the law of diminishing returns, adopted here in the particular version of diminishing returns to changing proportions.)

[7] Solow [24, p. 66].

series of other assumptions which Harrod and Domar *do not* make: a differentiable linear and homogeneous production function, perfect and infinite substitutability of labour and capital, perfect competition in the labour and in the capital markets, etc.. Moreover he makes the formidable assumption that there is only one commodity in the whole economic system. The extraordinary feature of these assumptions is that they are not only numerous, but peculiarly hybrid, opposite and extreme. On the one side the existence is assumed of only *one* commodity and on the other side the existence is assumed of an *infinite* number of techniques for producing it. On the one side the Keynesian view is accepted that the rate of interest has no importance in determining savings, and on the other side the opposite assumption is made that the rate of interest is so important as to be able to make the capital–output ratio vary from near zero to near infinity.

It is hard to see any rationale for this peculiar set of assumptions, except that of bringing in a particular shape of technology – and thus marginal productivity – at all costs, as the main determinant of income distribution and the rate of profit. It looks as if the marginal productivity theorists are willing to introduce almost any assumption, if it serves that purpose.

Ironically enough, the only really general results that could have been obtained from this analysis are very inimical to marginal productivities, as they do indeed refer to technology, but in a negative sense. Relation (vi.3.3) may be written as:

$$\frac{Y}{K} = \frac{1}{s} g_n , \qquad\qquad (\text{vi.4.1})$$

which is another simple equilibrium relation.[8] It states that, if $s$ and $g_n$ are constant, the equilibrium output to capital ratio (i.e. the reciprocal of the capital–output ratio), if it exists, is determined by the natural rate of growth divided by the over-all propensity to save, independently of

[8] It is significant that relation (vi.4.1) was not noticed by the original proponents of the marginal productivity approach. It is only when Meade [9] and Samuelson–Modigliani [21] discussed Pasinetti [13] that they discovered it. See below p. 131n. But by that time it had to be taken as a sort of lesser of two evils, as compared with (vi.2.3). Each of the two equilibrium growth relations (vi.2.3) and (vi.4.1) shows in fact a particular type of irrelevance of the production function in equilibrium growth. Expression (vi.2.3) shows that any production function is irrelevant for the determination of the equilibrium rate of profit when $s$ is taken as the variable, and expression (vi.4.1) shows that any production function is irrelevant for the determination of the equilibrium capital–output ratio when $\kappa$ is taken as the variable.

anything else, and therefore also independently of the shape of any 'production function' and of marginal productivities.[9]

## 5. *A first approximation synthesis*

But let us return to our main stream of argument. It may seem surprising at first that concentrating attention either on flexibility of $s$ or on flexibility of $\kappa$ should give rise to radically different conclusions on the determination of the rate of profit. Yet, in general, different assumptions do lead to different conclusions. The test of significance obviously lies in relaxing the original assumptions and seeing to what extent the previously reached conclusions stand or fall. This is precisely what will be done in the following pages. We shall be considering an economic system which has already reached full employment. The natural rate of growth $g_n$ will therefore be taken as given and constant. But no such restriction will be imposed on either $s$ or $\kappa$.

To begin with, flexibility of $s$ and flexibility of $\kappa$ must clearly be considered simultaneously. For, if it is at all justified to consider $s$ and $\kappa$ flexible, then it would be unjustified to consider them separately from each other. As a first approximation, we may start by keeping the simplifications of both sections 2 and 3 above, i.e. both the Classical simplification that $s_w = 0$ and the marginal productivity assumption that $\kappa$ may vary from zero to infinity.

The result is indeed interesting. By putting $s_w = 0$ and by writing $\kappa = K/Y$ in (VI.2.1), we obtain:

$$g_n \frac{K}{Y} = s_c \frac{P}{Y}. \qquad (\text{VI.5.1})$$

---

[9] It may also be interesting to notice that since, by definition,

$$\frac{P}{K} = \frac{P}{Y} \frac{Y}{K}, \qquad (1')$$

if one uses the most popular of all marginal-productivity production functions – the 'Cobb–Douglas' production function $Y = A K^{\alpha} L^{1-\alpha}$, where $\alpha$ is the constant share of profits in net national income – then substitution of $\alpha$ for $P/Y$ and of $g_n/s$ for $Y/K$ yields:

$$\frac{P}{K} = \frac{\alpha}{s} g_n, \qquad (2')$$

an expression which is 'almost' as simple as the Cambridge equation. This expression is of course much more general than the Cobb–Douglas production function, as it holds any time that the share of profits into income $\alpha$ can be taken as constant. If $\alpha$, $s$, $g_n$ are constant, the equilibrium rate of profit is determined by $(2')$ independently of anything else, and therefore also independently of marginal productivities.

126

Now we can see that – whether the capital–output ratio is fixed or variable – since $Y$ cancels out, we always obtain:

$$\frac{P}{K} = \frac{1}{s_c} g_n ,\qquad\text{(VI.5.2)}$$

i.e. the Cambridge equation! Thus, when jointly considered, the results of the Keynesian approach of section 2 prevail over the results of the marginal productivity approach of section 3. The equilibrium relations are such as to determine the rate of profit first of all, simply from $g_n$ and $s_c$, according to (VI.2.3), independently of anything else.

## 6. Irrelevance of the workers' propensity to save

We may now proceed to relaxing the Classical simplification that $s_w$ is zero. Suppose therefore that $s_w > 0$.

It is at this point that the basic contribution of Essay v may be brought in – a contribution that has come from the discovery of a fundamental relation (passed unnoticed in the whole of previous economic literature) which links profits to savings through the owner-ship of the capital stock. This relation simply follows from the insti-tutional principle that profits are distributed in proportion to the ownership of capital and that the ownership of capital derives from accumulated savings.

It may be useful to retrace the successive steps from which that rela-tion emerges. If capitalists have a positive saving propensity $s_c$ and workers also have a positive saving propensity $s_w$, in the long run, the capital stock owned by each category of savers becomes proportional to their savings, so that (using subscript $c$ for capitalists and $w$ for workers):

$$\frac{S}{K} = \frac{S_c}{K_c} = \frac{S_w}{K_w} .\qquad\text{(VI.6.1)}$$

But profits are also proportional to the capital stocks. If workers lend their capital to the capitalists and the assumption is made, for the time being, that the rate of interest on loans is equal to the rate of profit, then

$$\frac{P}{K} = \frac{P_c}{K_c} = \frac{P_w}{K_w} .\qquad\text{(VI.6.2)}$$

By dividing through we obtain:

$$\frac{P}{S} = \frac{P_c}{S_c} = \frac{P_w}{S_w} ,\qquad\text{(VI.6.3)}$$

or, since in equilibrium $I = S$,

$$\frac{P}{I} = \frac{P_c}{s_c P_c} = \frac{P_w}{s_w(W + P_w)}. \qquad (\text{VI}.6.4)$$

These are the basic relations from which the results of the previous essay may be deduced. If, in ($\text{VI}.6.4$), we consider the second equality first, we have $s_c P_w = s_w(W + P_w)$, which means that, in all equilibrium growth relations, workers' savings $s_w(W + P_w)$ always become equal to – and hence can be replaced by – $s_c P_w$ (i.e. the amount of savings the capitalists would do if workers' profits were to go to them). Hence $s_w$ drops out of all equilibrium relations and $s_c$ remains the only relevant saving propensity. If we now consider the first equality in ($\text{VI}.6.4$), by rearranging and dividing by $K$, we obtain:

$$\frac{P}{K} = \frac{1}{s_c} \frac{I}{K}, \qquad (\text{VI}.6.5)$$

or, since, in equilibrium growth, $(I/K) = g_n$,

$$\frac{P}{K} = \frac{1}{s_c} g_n. \qquad (\text{VI}.6.6)$$

As in the previous section therefore – but now *without* the restrictive simplification that $s_w = 0$ – the equilibrium rate of profit emerges as being determined by the natural rate of growth divided by the capitalists' propensity to save, independently of anything else.

The most remarkable feature of this relation is that the assumptions on which it has been derived are so few. This makes it a relation of the utmost generality. *As long as, in the economic system, there is a category of savers that save exclusively out of profit,* the only rate of profit that is compatible with equilibrium growth is the one given by the Cambridge equation, independently of anything else. It must be noticed that nothing has been said about the marginal productivity assumption of a capital–output ratio going from zero to infinity; for this assumption does not matter. In fact, *whatever assumption* is made on $\kappa$, it does not make any difference to the results. To conclude, although the Cambridge equation had originally been obtained on the assumptions of a constant $\kappa$ and a zero $s_w$, it emerges as being independent of both. Whether $\kappa$ is constant or variable, whether $s_w$ is zero or positive, the equilibrium rate of profit is determined by the natural rate of growth divided by the capitalists propensity to save.

## 7. *A marginal productivity escape route*

These results have come as a surprise to the marginal productivity theorists, who have reacted by calling them 'paradoxical'.[10]

It may be useful to consider the problem, for a moment, from a marginal productivity point of view. If we resume the relation of fig. VI.1, we can see that, at $r = (1/s_c)g_n$, the capital–output ratio is $\kappa^*$ (see fig. VI.2). Since $g_n \kappa^* = I/Y$, (VI.2.2) tells us that the range within which the system is operating is:

$$s_w < g_n \kappa^*. \qquad (\text{VI.7.1})$$

Now it can easily be seen that, within this range, the production function is entirely irrelevant. The capitalists' rate of capital accumulation is, by definition, $s_c P_c/K_c$. Therefore, if, *ex hypothesis*, $(P/K) > (1/s_c)g_n$, then $(s_c P_c/K_c) > g_n$, i.e. the capitalists would be accumulating faster than the rate of growth of the system, i.e. they would be increasing their share of total capital. But this is incompatible with equilibrium growth. Therefore the equilibrium rate of profit can never be higher than $(1/s_c)g_n$. It also follows from figs. VI.1 and VI.2 that the equilibrium capital–output ratio can never be lower than $\kappa^*$. Thus the whole stretch of the curve to the right of $r = (1/s_c)g_n$ is irrelevant. (In fig. VI.2, it has been drawn as a broken line.)

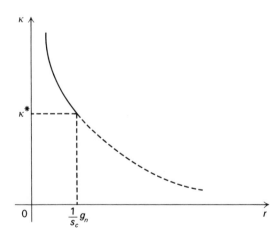

Fig. VI.2

---

[10] The term is Samuelson's, who has used it on two different occasions: [21], [17], which have in common the feature of revealing relations that are contrary to marginal productivity theory.

We can now see what the 'paradox' is for marginal productivity theorists. All extreme assumptions had been made to render marginal productivity relevant; and yet such assumptions turn out to be, so to speak, 'frustrated'. The production function is supposed to exist, to be 'well-behaved', differentiable and all the rest; and yet, beyond the point $r = (1/s_c)g_n$, it is *as if* it did not exist. The capital–output ratio is supposed to be perfectly flexible and even to be susceptible of going down asymptotically to zero; and yet, below the level $\kappa^*$, it cannot fall. It is *as if* it were fixed at $\kappa^*$.

It is natural at this point to investigate the meaning of range (VI.7.1). This can be done usefully by examining the effects of a positive $s_w$. Workers' propensity to save $s_w$ has no effect on the equilibrium rate of profit, as we have seen, but it does have an effect on the share of total capital owned by the workers. As can easily be obtained,[11] in equilibrium:

$$\frac{K_w}{K} = \frac{s_w(s_c - g_n \kappa^*)}{(s_c - s_w)g_n \kappa^*}; \qquad \frac{K_c}{K} = \frac{(g_n \kappa^* - s_w)s_c}{(s_c - s_w)g_n \kappa^*}, \qquad (\text{VI.7.2})$$

where $\kappa^*$ is the capital–output ratio corresponding to $r = (1/s_c)g_n$. The higher is $s_w$ the greater is the fraction of total capital owned by the workers. When $s_w = 0$, then $(K_w/K) = 0$ and $(K_c/K) = 1$ – the whole capital stock is owned by the capitalists. When $0 < s_w < g_n \kappa^*$, then $0 < (K_c/K) < 1$ – the capital stock is owned partly by the capitalists and partly by the workers. Finally when $s_w = g_n \kappa^*$, the extreme case is reached in which $(K_w/K) = 1$ and $(K_c/K) = 0$ – the whole capital stock is owned by the workers and the capitalists have been eliminated from the system. This precisely corresponds to the upper limit of range (VI.7.1).

To the marginal productivity theorists this has suggested an escape route. If the capitalists were not to exist any more, their propensity to save obviously could not determine the rate of profit. There *is*, therefore, a way of preventing the Cambridge equation from operating, and that is by eliminating the capitalists from the system! The marginal productivity theorists have concentrated on this case. If:

$$s_w \geq g_n \kappa^*, \qquad (\text{VI.7.3})$$

workers' saving propensity is so high as to allow them to accumulate faster than the capitalists, at a rate of profit lower than $r = (1/s_c)g_n$. The share of workers' capital in total capital will increase indefinitely and tend asymptotically to unity. The workers will eventually dominate the economy and the capitalists will become irrelevant – a 'euthanasia'

---

[11] An expression for $K_w/K$ appears already on p. 108 above. By substituting $I/Y$ with $g_n \kappa^*$, (VI.7.2) is obtained.

of the capitalists. In such an eventual state, only one category of savers is left – the workers – and marginal productivity theorists can retreat back to the analysis of section 3 above, though with an economic system restricted to operate only in the upper part of the $\kappa$–$r$ relationship (the continuous line in fig. VI.2). Since there is only one category of savers, the equilibrium capital–output ratio, in the upper part of fig. VI.2, is determined independently of the shape of technology, according to (VI.3.3), which in this case becomes:

$$\kappa = \frac{s_w}{g_n}. \qquad (\text{VI.7.4})$$

But the important point, for the marginal productivity theorists, concerns the rate of profit. They have claimed that, at capital–output ratio (VI.7.4), the rate of profit is determined by the marginal productivity of capital[12, 13].

The conclusion may appear attractive, but the whole analysis is still lame. While the assumption of a zero workers' propensity to save has been relaxed, the extreme assumption of an infinitely flexible capital–output ratio is still being kept. This did not matter as long as the capitalists had not been considered as eliminated from the system. For, with both capitalists and workers co-existing, it does not make any difference which assumption is made on the shape of technology. But as soon as one wants to analyse a situation in which *technology* does become relevant, then clearly, on technology itself, one cannot accept any arbitrary assumption. One must investigate first the relation, if there is any, between technology and the rate of profit.

[12] See Meade [9] and Samuelson–Modigliani [21]. Both Meade and Samuelson–Modigliani have insisted on formal symmetry. Their argument runs roughly as follows: If $s_w < g_n \kappa^*$ then the Cambridge equation holds, if on the other hand $s_w > g_n \kappa^*$, then the marginal productivity results hold (Samuelson–Modigliani call $s_w < g_n \kappa^*$ the 'primal' or 'Pasinetti' range and $s_w > g_n \kappa^*$ the 'dual' or 'anti-Pasinetti' range). I have pointed out already, in [14], [15], [16], that this procedure is inaccurate and misleading. If $s_w < g_n \kappa^*$, the Cambridge equation does hold indeed *irrespective of any assumption on technology;* but if $s_w > g_n \kappa^*$, what happens depends crucially on technology. The Meade–Samuelson–Modigliani's marginal productivity results only follow on particular and unacceptable assumptions on technology – as will appear on the following pages.

[13] The real paradox, it seems to me, is that marginal productivity theory was successful mainly because it could be used to support the legitimacy of a rate of profit in a capitalist system. To salvage the theory at all costs, its supporters are now compelled to rely on a classless society, in which the capitalists do not exist any more and the workers have taken over the ownership of the whole capital stock.

## 8. *The workers' savings required for the disappearance of the capitalists*

Before proceeding further, it may be interesting to ask a concrete question. In formal terms, to write $s_w > g_n \kappa^*$ does not look any less plausible than to write $s_w < g_n \kappa^*$. But, on concrete terms, we may ask: how much saving would the workers have to do in order to be able to accumulate faster than the capitalists and eventually eliminate them from the economic system? The answer is simple and straightforward: the workers would have to provide all the savings that are needed for full employment growth. If – as is generally observed in industrialized countries – the proportion of net national income that is invested (and saved) is of an order of magnitude of 15 per cent, then we may roughly say that workers propensity to save $s_w$ would have to exceed the figure of 15 per cent for the workers to be able to end up eventually owning the whole capital stock.[14]

There is no indication that the workers' propensity to save will get anywhere near 15 per cent in the foreseeable future. Consequently, there is no *practical* reason to worry about capitalists' 'euthanasia'. Yet the case may be interesting from an analytical point of view.

## 9. *Capital–output ratio and rate of profit*

It becomes necessary, at this stage, to discuss the relation between technology and the rate of profit, in order to see whether there is any justification for the extreme marginal–productivity assumption that the capital–output ratio is an inverse monotonic function of the rate of profit that goes from near zero to near infinity.

[14] I mentioned this figure already (or, to be precise, a figure between 12 per cent and 16 per cent) in my [16, p. 304], as against the figure of 5 per cent given by Samuelson–Modigliani [21, p. 274]. In their reply, Samuelson–Modigliani skilfully avoid mentioning their own – obviously inconsistent – figure of 5 per cent and go on to discuss implications for $s_c$, which had not been under discussion at all. Their only objection to my figure of 15 per cent is that I would be 'taking as already proven the very proposition that is under debate, to wit, that the economies from which we draw these estimates of $I/Y$ are in fact in Pasinetti golden age equilibrium' [22, p. 329]. But this is nonsense. If an economy with $(I/Y) = 15$ per cent were not in a 'Pasinetti golden age' and were instead in what Samuelson–Modigliani call 'anti-Pasinetti' or 'dual golden age', then $(I/Y) = 15$ per cent would precisely imply $s_w = 15$ per cent. If, on the other hand, an economy with the same $(I/Y) = 15$ per cent were in a 'Pasinetti golden age', then $s_w$ would have to be even higher than 15 per cent in order for the workers to be able to eventually eliminate the capitalists. (Samuelson–Modigliani have perhaps overlooked the fact that their own 'anti-Pasinetti golden age' requires a higher, not a lower, capital–output ratio than their 'Pasinetti golden age'.)

132

Now it so happens that the relation of the capital–output ratio (and the capital–labour ratio) to the rate of profit has been the subject of an intense discussion in the recent economic literature – see [17] – and that something entirely new has emerged on this matter. As is well known by now, the formerly well established belief that the capital–output ratio is an inverse monotonic function of the rate of profit has been shown to be entirely without foundation. One thing, therefore, we can be sure of from the start, and that is that the relation between $\kappa$ and $r$ is *not* of the shape the marginal productivity theorists have supposed it to be (i.e. of the shape represented in figs. VI.1 and VI.2 above). The capital–output ratio does, of course, depend on the rate of profit for many reasons. As the rate of profit changes: (i) the technique of production may change, (ii) even if the technique of production remains the same, all relative prices change, (iii) the composition of output, and thus of the capital stock may change too. However, nothing can be said *a priori* on the direction of any of these changes. If we represent the relation between the capital–output ratio $\kappa$ and the rate of profit $r$ by:

$$\kappa = \varphi(r), \qquad (\text{VI.9.1})$$

we can say that nothing is known in general on the shape of this function. The relevant properties of $\varphi(r)$ can only be stated in negative terms. In general, this function is not monotonic, is not smoothly differentiable and, most of all, has finite limits above and below. In other words, there is a maximum $\kappa_{max}$ and a minimum $\kappa_{min}$ above which and below which, respectively, the capital–output ratio does not go. This is important for our purposes: the capital–output ratio can only vary within a finite band.

In the Harrod–Domar original formulation, for simplicity, $\kappa_{max}$ and $\kappa_{min}$ are supposed to coincide and the finite band reduces to just a horizontal line. This may well be too simple. But it is one thing to object that $\kappa$ may not be absolutely constant, and may move in a finite band; and an entirely different thing to strain exasperatedly such a band (as the marginal productivity theorists have done) and make it cover the whole positive quadrant from zero to infinity.

Clearly, the appropriate question to ask is: how wide is that band likely to be? Now, although this question cannot be answered in general (discussion [17] reveals that $\kappa$ may go up or down but cannot obviously indicate in general by how much), yet a whole series of relevant remarks can be made. It must be stressed that, up to a short while ago, it was believed that $\kappa$ *always* goes down as $r$ goes up (and this made it appear reasonable on ground of mathematical convenience to use a function of the type of figs. VI.1 and VI.2). But our knowledge has been changed radically by discussions [17]. Not only do we know that κ may go up or down, as the rate of profit changes, but we also know that it does so for hundreds of commodities and industries so that many of these changes can be expected to cancel each other out. There is in fact no reason to believe that the capital–output ratio should be lower or higher at the minimum rate of profit $r = 0$ than it is at the maximum rate of profit $r = Y/K$. This alone shows dramatically how misleading marginal productivity analysis must be in assuming that κ always tends to infinity at $r = 0$ and to zero at $r = Y/K$.

Surely when it is known that a certain magnitude is influenced by hundreds of effects in opposite directions, the most reasonable assumption to make, *if an assumption is to be made at all*, is that all these effects will tend to cancel each other out. In other words, when the rate of profit changes, the most reasonable assumption to make on κ is, after all, Harrod–Domar original assumption that κ will remain constant![15]

If we do make this assumption of a constant κ, the answer to our problems becomes very simple. We have $\kappa^* = \bar{\kappa}$ and we have that no κ exists higher than $\kappa^* = \bar{\kappa}$. Therefore, either $s_w < \bar{\kappa}\, g_n$, and in this case equilibrium growth is possible, with the Cambridge equation determining the rate of profit; or else $s_w > g_n\, \bar{\kappa}$, and in this case no equilibrium growth is possible at all. In between the Cambridge-equation equilibrium range and the no-equilibrium range, there remains the singular point $s_w = g_n\, \bar{\kappa}$ at which a 'knife-edge' Harrodian equilibrium growth path is possible, with the workers owning the whole capital stock, the capitalists being eliminated from the system and the rate of profit being indeterminate. But such a 'knife-edge' growth path is one of no practical relevance.

## 10. *The case of a highly flexible capital–output ratio*

But let us suppose a case, for the sake of analysis, in which not only is κ not absolutely constant but actually (as a function of the rate of profit) varies within an exceptionally wide band. Samuelson and Modigliani, in their [21] provide such an example. They abandon the marginal

[15] Keynes made us realize that traditional economic theory had greatly exaggerated the influence of the rate of interest on savings, and thus of its equilibrating power through variations of investments. Similarly the recent discussions on the re-switching of techniques [17] should make us realize that traditional economics has also greatly exaggerated the influence of the rate of interest (and of profit) on the choice of techniques and thus of its equilibrating power through variations in the capital–output ratio.

productivity relation of figs. VI.1 and VI.2, and hypothesize the particular function $\varphi(r)$ which is here represented in fig. VI.3.[16] It must be noticed that in spite of the authors' disclaimer[17], such a function still envinces most of the prejudices coming from marginal productivity theory: the range of variation of $\kappa$ goes from $\kappa_{max} \simeq 12.5$ to $\kappa_{min} \simeq 3.2$ (i.e. $\kappa_{max}$ is supposed to be 4 times larger than $\kappa_{min}$). Moreover $\kappa_{max}$ is supposed to obtain at $r = 0$ and $\kappa_{min}$ at $r = Y/K$. Furthermore the function is supposed to be monotonically decreasing for all relevant purposes (the only little bit of it which is not so is relegated to that part of the curve which is not relevant anyhow).[18] Yet let us consider this case.

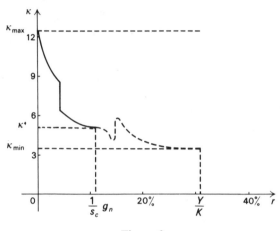

Fig. VI.3

First of all we can say immediately – since this is true in general – that the equilibrium rate of profit cannot be higher than the one determined by the Cambridge equation. Hence that part of the function $\varphi(r)$ which is on the right of $r = (1/s_c)g_n$ (the broken line in fig. VI.3) is irrelevant as far as the determination of the rate of profit is concerned.

[16] The curve of fig. VI.3 is obtained from Samuelson–Modigliani's fig. 1 [22, p. 323], where they represent the *reciprocal* of $\kappa$ as a function of $r$.

[17] 'We have made it' – they claim – 'as "pathological" and "ill-behaved" as we could think of' (Samuelson–Modigliani [22, p. 322]). Incidentally, it is not clear why the function of fig. VI.3 or any non-monotonic function, should be 'pathological' and 'ill-behaved', unless one decides so to call any function that gives trouble to marginal productivity theory.

[18] It may be interesting to compare the shape of Samuelson–Modigliani's curve with that used at least by another author. In his [12], Morishima considers a two-commodity four-technique economy in which the $\varphi(r)$ function that is obtained is the

This means that as long as:

$$\frac{s_w}{g_n} < \kappa^* , \qquad (\text{VI}.10.1)$$

both capitalists and workers coexist in the system, and the only type of equilibrium growth that is possible is of the 'Cambridge equation' type.

Secondly, if:

$$\frac{s_w}{g_n} > \kappa^* , \qquad (\text{VI}.10.2)$$

at least two sub-cases must be distinguished. If:

$$\frac{s_w}{g_n} > \kappa_{max} , \qquad (\text{VI}.10.3)$$

then no equilibrium growth is possible at all. (This range corresponds to the range $(s_w/g_n) > \bar{\kappa}$ in the Harrod–Domar case of a constant $\kappa$.) But in between the 'Cambridge-equation' equilibrium range and the no-equilibrium range, there is a range of capital–output ratios (which may be wider than the singular point $\bar{\kappa}$ in the Harrod–Domar case), in which, if $s_w/g_n$ happens to fall, i.e.

$$\kappa^* \leq \frac{s_w}{g_n} \leq \kappa_{max} , \qquad (\text{VI}.10.4)$$

then workers' savings are such as to make it possible for them to take over the whole capital stock, and thus become the only category of

following (see fig. VI.4):

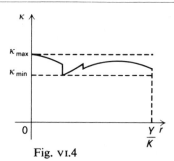

Fig. VI.4

(This curve, though not drawn explicitly by Morishima, is implicit in his fig. 3 [12, pp. 36 and 39], where $\kappa$ is the slope of the straight line joining each point of the discontinuous curve to the origin, while $r$ is on the horizontal axis.) It is significant that Morishima, who has obviously drawn his curve without thinking of the implications for traditional theory (unlike Samuelson–Modigliani), should arrive at a curve – fig. VI.4 above – which has no likeness whatever with the marginal productivity relation of figs. VI.1 and VI.2 above.

savers in the economic system. Within (VI.10.4), since $g_n$ and $s_w$ are fixed, the equilibrium capital–output ratio is determined by general relation (VI.3.3), independently of anything else, i.e., in our case:

$$\kappa = \frac{s_w}{g_n}.$$ (VI.10.5)

Then, at this capital–output ratio, the rate of profit compatible with it is given by the inverse function $\varphi^{-1}$, i.e.

$$r = \varphi^{-1}(s_w/g_n).$$ (VI.10.6)

Thus, within the range (VI.10.4), an equilibrium growth is in fact possible at capital–output ratio (VI.10.5) and at rate of profit (VI.10.6).

It must be noticed that (VI.10.6) has nothing any more to do with marginal productivities, and that it represents in fact a very peculiar, and rather evanescent, way of determining the rate of profit.[19] It yields a unique solution for $r$ only if $\varphi(r)$ is monotonically decreasing between $r = 0$ and $r = (1/s_c)g_n$, as Samuelson and Modigliani have supposed it to be. But there is no reason why it should be so. With a non-monotonic $\varphi(r)$, the solutions for $r$ will in general be multiple.[20] And the number of multiple solutions is likely to be higher and higher, the more frequent are the oscillations of $\varphi(r)$, and the narrower is the range (VI.10.4). In the limit, i.e. in the Harrod–Domar case of a constant $\kappa$, multiplicity becomes infinite at the singular point $\bar\kappa = s_w/g_n$, i.e. solutions (VI.10.6) become indeterminate.

It is important to notice that, in any case, whether the solutions are unique, multiple or infinite (i.e. indeterminate), they are bounded within very definite limits. For, the rate of profit cannot be higher than the one given by the Cambridge equation. In other words, in all cases, $r$ is always

$$r \le \frac{1}{s_c}\, g_n.$$ (VI.10.7)

Thus, even in the peculiar case of a highly flexible capital–output ratio, coupled with the peculiar case of an economic system in which $s_w$ is so high as to make it end up with one class of savers – the workers – the 'Cambridge equation' always sets an upper bound to the equilibrium rate of profit.

[19] No author that I know of has ever used such a peculiar way of determining the rate of profit, except in polemics with, and as a way of claiming limitations to, the 'Cambridge equation'.

[20] In Morishima's case of fig. VI.4 above – a two-commodity four-technique economy – such solutions for $r$ will normally be multiple.

## 11. *Conclusions for the general case*

It is important to realize that the relevance (or rather the irrelevance) of the range of variation of $\kappa$, on which the marginal productivity theorists have pinned all their hopes, depends not only on the sensitivity of $\kappa$ to changes in $r$ (or variability of $\kappa$ on the vertical axis). It also depends on the width of the field over which $r$ itself is allowed to vary on the horizontal axis. For, clearly, the shorter the stretch over which $r$ is allowed to vary on the horizontal axis, the smaller the variation of $\varphi(r)$ that can be expected, *even if* the function itself were to be very sensitive to large changes in $r$.

We have seen already in the previous pages that the equilibrium rate of profit can never go beyond the point $r = (1/s_c)g_n$. And this means immediately that the major part of the function $\varphi(r)$ is irrelevant in any case. But we may now ask whether there might also be a lower point below which the equilibrium rate of profit cannot fall. And the answer is that there is. In any capitalist system, the equilibrium rate of profit cannot fall at or below the level of the rate of economic growth,[21] i.e.

$$g_n < r. \tag{VI.11.1}$$

This chops off as irrelevant another stretch of the function $\varphi(r)$. Thus, even in the case – as the one hypothesized by Samuelson and Modigliani – of a capital–output ratio exceptionally sensitive to changes in $r$, since the relevant field of variation of $r$ is severely restricted to:

$$g_n < r \leq \frac{1}{s_c} g_n, \tag{VI.11.2}$$

the capital–output ratio cannot be expected to vary substantially. Fig. VI.5 illustrates the necessarily limited variability of the Samuelson-Modigliani capital–output ratio in the narrow interval (VI.11.2). The point is that only a small fraction of the total field of possible variation of $\kappa$ is relevant.[22]

[21] In the particular case of a hypothetical economic system in which the workers have taken over the ownership of the whole capital stock, a rate of profit lower than the rate of growth would mean that individuals *permanently* contribute to production, in the form of savings, more than what they receive in the form of profit. Such a state of affairs could not persist. People would soon discover they are better off by not saving at all.

[22] It may be useful to point out that in Samuelson–Modigliani's diagrams [22, pp. 325, 328], what they call the 'dual' or 'anti-Pasinetti' range is always drawn as including not only the Samuelson–Modigliani range proper (which is very small), but also the no equilibrium range (which is enormously wide). This is inaccurate. The no-equilibrium range does not belong to the 'Pasinetti range' but does not belong to the 'anti-Pasinetti range' either.

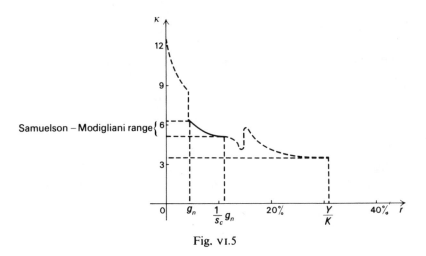

Fig. vi.5

The idea of a 'knife-edge' therefore comes back after all. It may well be a blunt, rather than a sharp, knife-edge, and it is a severely truncated one.

The conclusion, therefore, is not much different from the one already reached at the end of section 9 for the simplified case of a constant $\kappa$. Either the workers' propensity to save $s_w$ does not reach the critical level beyond which the workers would accumulate faster than the capitalists, and in this case equilibrium growth is possible, with the Cambridge equation determining the rate of profit. Or else $s_w$ is higher than that level, and in this case what will normally happen is that no equilibrium growth is possible at all. In between the Cambridge-equation equilibrium range and the no-equilibrium range, there is a small range of values for $s_w$ for which an equilibrium growth path of the Harrodian type is possible but is likely to be of no practical relevance. In any case, even if such a growth path were to be realized, the equilibrium rate of profit could not be higher than the one determined by the Cambridge equation.

## 12. *Rate of interest and rate of profit*

The foregoing analysis may be generalized further. The assumption, kept so far, of a rate of interest exactly equal to the rate of profit is in fact not necessary. This may be realized by a more careful consideration of the fundamental relations (vi.6.1)–(vi.6.4).

Suppose that the workers lend their savings to the capitalists and

139

receive interest according to a rate of interest $i = P_w/K_w$, which is lower than the rate of profit the capitalists obtain. If we go back to the relation (v1.6.1), we may realize that such relation holds independently of whether the rates of profit and of interest are uniform or differentiated. And since, in equilibrium, $I = S$ and $(I/K) = g_n$, it follows immediately from (v1.6.1) that:

$$\frac{P_c}{K_c} = \frac{1}{s_c} g_n. \qquad (\text{v}_1.12.1)$$

This expression represents in fact a more general version of the 'Cambridge equation'. It shows that the natural rate of growth and the capitalists propensity to save determine the rate of profit on capitalists' capital first of all, independently of anything else, and therefore also independently of the rate of interest.[23]

In the previous pages the particular case has been considered in which the rate of interest is equal to the rate of profit, and therefore $i$ coincides with (v1.12.1). Now let us consider the more general case in which the rate of interest is proportional to, but lower than, the rate of profit the capitalists obtain on their capital. Suppose that the coefficient of proportionality is $\mu$. Then:

$$i = \mu \frac{P_c}{K_c} = \mu \frac{1}{s_c} g_n, \qquad \text{where } \mu < 1. \qquad (\text{v}_1.12.2)$$

When this is the case, total profits will accrue to the capital owners according to two different rates: a rate of profit (v1.12.1) on capitalists' capital and a rate of interest (v1.12.2) on workers' capital lent to the capitalists.

What in Essay v has been called the over-all rate of profit is, however, neither (v1.12.1) nor (v1.12.2), but:

$$\frac{P}{K} = \frac{P_w + P_c}{K_w + K_c}, \qquad (\text{v}_1.12.3)$$

i.e. the ratio of the sum of total income accruing to capital owners (whether in the form of interest or in the form of profits) to total capital. Therefore $P/K$ will fall in between $P_c/K_c$ and $i$, i.e.

$$\frac{P_c}{K_c} \geq \frac{P}{K} \geq i, \qquad (\text{v}_1.12.4)$$

[23] I myself did not come to this result until after the publication of [13], in a discussion with Amit Bhaduri. But other authors have arrived at it independently. See Laing [5].

and will obviously be a weighted average of $P_c/K_c$ and $i$, the weights being represented by the share of total capital owned by the capitalists and the share of total capital owned by the workers respectively – expressions (vi.7.2). Let us write:

$$\frac{P}{K} = \frac{P_c}{K_c}\frac{K_c}{K} + i\,\frac{K_w}{K}. \qquad (\text{vi.12.5})$$

We may now notice that expressions (vi.7.2), for $K_c/K$ and $K_w/K$, do contain $s_w$ and this means that $s_w$ contributes to determining how near $P/K$ is to $P_c/K_c$ or to $i$. However, both $P_c/K_c$ and $i$ are independent of $s_w$.

Clearly, we may always write:

$$\frac{P}{K} = \frac{1}{\gamma s_c}\,g_n, \qquad \text{where } \gamma \geq 1, \qquad (\text{vi.12.6})$$

and we may easily find, from (vi.12.1), (vi.12.2), (vi.7.2), that:

$$\gamma = \frac{g_n\,\kappa^*(s_c - s_w)}{g_n\,\kappa^*(s_c - \mu\,s_w) - s_c s_w(1 - \mu)}. \qquad (\text{vi.12.7})$$

When either $\mu = 1$ or $s_w = 0$, then $\gamma = 1$, and we are back to the previous results. But when $\mu < 1$ and $s_w > 0$, then $\gamma > 1$.

The interest of (vi.12.6) is that it shows that $\gamma$ comes to reinforce $s_c$. A rate of interest lower than the rate of profit has the same effect as a higher propensity to save of the capitalists, as it redistributes income in favour of the workers.

## 13. *Many groups of savers*

As already mentioned in Essay v, the analysis may also be generalized to many groups of savers. We may subdivide capitalists and workers into as many groups as is necessary. Suppose that there are $N$ groups of capitalists, characterized by different propensities to save: $s_{c1} > s_{c2} > \ldots s_{cN}$. It can be seen immediately that only one group of capitalists will eventually dominate the equilibrium growth path. For, as soon as more than one group of capitalists is introduced into relation (vi.6.1), the growth rate of the capital stock owned by the thriftiest group emerges as being higher than the growth rate of any other capitalists' group. Therefore, growth being exponential, the thriftiest group of capitalists will in the end dominate all the others. Only the highest among the capitalists' propensities to save listed above, namely $s_{c1}$, is therefore relevant for the problem of determining the rate of profit that will eventually characterize the equilibrium growth path. The whole previous analysis merely needs being reinterpreted in the sense of reading $s_{c1}$ for $s_c$, i.e. of reinterpreting $s_c$ as representing the propensity to save of the thriftiest group of capitalists.[24]

Suppose moreover that there are $M$ groups of workers, also characterized by different propensities to save: $s_{w1} > s_{w2} > \ldots > s_{wM} \geq 0$. Here, as usual, the conclusions are radically different. The introduction of more than one group of workers into relation (VI.6.1) does not prevent each group from achieving the same equilibrium rate of capital accumulation as all the others. The effect of different propensities to save here is that of determining a different equilibrium share, into the ownership of the total capital stock, for each of the workers' groups.[25] All groups of workers (no matter how different their propensities to save) will therefore coexist on the equilibrium growth path.

An important implication of this is that the crucial propensity to save that delimits the range beyond which the workers would accumulate faster than the capitalists is the *weighted average* of all the workers' propensities to save (i.e. the average of the $M$ propensities to save $s_{w1}, s_{w2}, \ldots s_{wM}$, each of them weighted according to the fraction of the income of the corresponding group into total workers' income). Therefore, if we denote by $s_{w*}$ this weighted average of workers' propensity to save, we may conclude that we only have to substitute $s_{w*}$ for $s_w$ in all the inequalities of the previous sections.[26]

---

[24] This comes to strengthen the arguments of the previous sections 10 and 11. The higher the relevant capitalists' propensity to save, the shorter is the relevant range of possible variability of $r$ (and therefore of $\kappa$) in fig. VI.5 above.

[25] As may easily be checked, by using the same procedure as the one used for (VI.7.2), the equilibrium shares (supposing for simplicity uniform rates of profit on all capital stocks) emerge as:

$$\frac{K_{wi}}{K} = \frac{\lambda_i s_{wi} (s_c - \kappa^* g_n)}{(s_c - s_{wi})\kappa^* g_n}, \quad i = 1, 2, \ldots, M,$$

where $\lambda_i$ is the proportion of the number of workers in group $i$ ($i = 1, 2, \ldots, M$) to the total number of workers, so that $\sum_{i=1}^{M} \lambda_i = 1$.

[26] Here again Samuelson and Modigliani have been betrayed by their enthusiasm for symmetry. In their 'general theorem' concerning many groups of savers, after correctly stating that only the highest among the capitalists' propensities to save is the relevant one, they (erroneously) single out the highest of the workers' propensities to save (instead of the weighted average of *all* of them) as the saving propensity to use in the two inequalities defining their 'Pasinetti range' and 'anti-Pasinetti range'. See a correction by Vaughan [27].

## 14. *Further extensions*

Among the further extensions that are possible, I shall only mention here the elaborations that can be pursued by introducing the hypothesis that the process of production is carried out by corporations with an independently given retention ratio (the ratio of retained to total profits) as against the saving propensities of the various groups of families, who receive profit incomes and/or wage incomes. This field of analysis is wide open for investigation[27] and I shall not enter into it, lest I make the present essay impossibly long.

## 15. *A socialist economy*

Of particular interest to our purposes is, however, the case in which the crucial propensity to save $s_c$ is equal to unity. This cannot, of course, happen in a capitalist economy, but can be obtained in a socialist system, where the responsibility for carrying out the production process and the direct ownership of the means of production are taken over by the State, which as such cannot consume.[28] In this case the crucial propensity to save $s_c$ becomes unity as an institutional property, so that even the remaining assumption of a constant proportion of profits saved is removed. (Incidentally it may be noticed that precisely in this case in which all the capitalists have indeed been eliminated, the Samuelson–Modigliani range in fig. VI.5 reduces to one single point, i.e. to complete irrelevance, whatever be the relation $\kappa = \varphi(r)$.)

When $s_c = 1$, the Cambridge equation reduces to the simple equality of the equilibrium rate of profit to the natural rate of growth:

$$\frac{P}{K} = g_n , \qquad\qquad (\text{VI}.15.1)$$

---

[27] See particularly: Kaldor [4], Pettenati [18], Marris [7], Wood [28].

[28] To this association of $s_c = 1$ with the case of a socialist system, Samuelson–Modigliani have objected that 'the government uses resources to provide many kinds of current services which it could finance with its property income ... it could always distribute some of its property income by gratuitous transfers' [22, p. 286]. But this is (implicitly) assuming that all the State revenue should be 'property income'. Such an assumption is entirely unwarranted. There is no reason why, in a socialist system, all State services and transfers should be financed in a way proportional to capital. The comparison of socialist and capitalist systems refers here to the production activity. If one wants to introduce other activities, (taxation, transfers, services of various kind) one may of course do so, but one must make comparable assumptions for socialist and for capitalist systems. See on this, for example, Steedman [25].

which I have called the 'natural' rate of profit. As already pointed out in Essay v, the implication of this is that workers may be left entirely free to save whatever proportion of their incomes they may choose. If the Central Authority borrows such savings and pays a rate of interest equal to the natural rate of profit, then, in equilibrium growth, the total amount of workers' savings turns out to be exactly equal to the total amount of the interest paid to them. Total consumption turns out to be equal to total wages and total investments turn out to be equal to total profits, although wages and interest are partly consumed and partly saved. An economic system which is on such a growth path therefore possesses all the normative properties of the economic systems in which total wages are equal to total consumption.[29] At the natural rate of profit, the techniques that are chosen yield the highest per-capita consumption. The 'natural' rate of profit is therefore an *efficient* rate of profit.

It is remarkable that the efficient case should be the clearest one, from an analytical point of view. It relies on a minimum of assumptions, it contains a minimum of complications and evinces the maximum of simplicity.

## 16. *The rate of profit in an expanding economy*

One final remark is required by way of conclusion.

For more than a century now, since the time of Marx and Böhm-Bawerk, economic theorists have been debating whether the rate of profit is due to any 'productivity' of capital and whether capital can in any sense be said to be 'productive'. But new horizons have been opened. In the long run, if full employment and full capacity utilization are to be kept, the rate of profit is determined by the natural rate of growth divided by the capitalists' propensity to save, independently of any 'productivity' of capital (no matter how it may be defined) and indeed independently of anything else. The most surprising outcome of all is that the long-run rate of profit is even independent of 'capital'! In the long run, capital itself becomes a variable; and it is capital that has to be adapted to an exogenously determined rate of profit, not the other way round.

---

[29] On the normative properties of the case $s_c = 1$, see, for example, Sato [23], Balestra–Baranzini [1].

The theoretical foundations are seen at their clearest when the relations are stripped down to their essentials – i.e. in the purest case in which $s_c = 1$ and therefore $(P/K) = g_n \equiv n + \lambda$. The rate of profit is determined, fundamentally, not by the 'quantity of capital', but by the rates of growth of labour and of the productivity of labour.

*REFERENCES*

[1]   Balestra, Piero, and Baranzini, Mauro, 'Some Optimal Aspects in a Two Class Growth Model with a Differentiated Interest Rate', *Kyklos*, 1971, pp. 240–56.

[2]   Kahn, Richard F., 'Exercises in the Analysis of Growth', *Oxford Economic Papers*, 1959, pp. 143–56.

[3]   Kaldor, Nicholas, 'Alternative Theories of Distribution', *The Review of Economic Studies*, 1955–6, pp. 83–100.

[4]   —— 'Marginal Productivity and the Macroeconomic Theories of Distribution: Comment on Samuelson and Modigliani', *The Review of Economic Studies*, 1966, pp. 309–19.

[5]   Laing, N. F., 'Two Notes on Pasinetti's Theorem', *The Economic Record*, 1969, pp. 373–85.

[6]   Maneschi, Andrea, 'The Existence of a Two-class Economy in Kaldor's and Pasinetti's Model of Growth and Distribution', *The Review of Economic Studies*, January 1974, pp. 149–50.

[7]   Marris, R. L., 'Why Economics needs a Theory of the Firm', *The Economic Journal*, 1972, pp. 321–52.

[8]   Meade, J. E., *A Neoclassical Theory of Economic Growth*, London, 1961.

[9]   —— 'The Rate of Profit in a Growing Economy', *The Economic Journal*, 1963, pp. 665–74.

[10]  Meade, J. E. and Hahn, F. H., 'The Rate of Profit in a Growing Economy', *The Economic Journal*, 1965, pp. 445–8.

[11]  Meade, J. E., 'The Outcome of the Pasinetti Process: a Note', *The Economic Journal*, 1966, pp. 161–5.

[12]  Morishima, Michio, *Theory of Economic Growth*, Oxford, 1969.

[13]  Pasinetti, Luigi L., 'Rate of Profit and Income Distribution in relation to the Rate of Economic Growth', *The Review of Economic Studies*, 1962, pp. 267–79, reprinted here on pp. 103–20.

[14]  —— 'Professor Meade's Rate of Profit in a Growing Economy', *The Economic Journal*, 1964, pp. 488–9.

[15] —— 'The Rate of Profit in a Growing Economy: a Reply', *The Economic Journal*, 1966, pp. 158–60.

[16] —— 'New Results in an Old Framework: Comment on Samuelson and Modigliani', *The Review of Economic Studies*, 1966, pp. 303–6.

[17] —— 'Changes in the Rate of Profit and Switches of Technique', *The Quarterly Journal of Economics*, November 1966, pp. 503–17. See also the ensuing discussion, under the heading 'Paradoxes in Capital Theory: A Symposium' by Samuelson, Levhari, Morishima, Bruno-Burmeister-Sheshinski, Garegnani, in the same issue of *The Quarterly Journal of Economics*.

[18] Pettenati, Paolo, 'Il teorema di Pasinetti in un diverso quadro di riferimento', *Studi economici*, 1967, pp. 581–8.

[19] Robinson, Joan, *The Accumulation of Capital*, London, 1956.

[20] —— 'Comment on Samuelson and Modigliani', *The Review of Economic Studies*, 1966, pp. 307–8.

[21] Samuelson, Paul, A., and Modigliani, Franco, 'The Pasinetti Paradox in Neoclassical and More General Models', *The Review of Economic Studies*, 1966, pp. 269–301.

[22] —— 'Reply to Pasinetti and Robinson', *The Review of Economic Studies*, 1966, pp. 321–30.

[23] Sato, K., 'The Neoclassical Theorem and Distribution of Income and Wealth', *The Review of Economic Studies*, 1966, pp. 331–5.

[24] Solow, Robert M., 'A Contribution to the Theory of Economic Growth', *The Quarterly Journal of Economics*, 1956, pp. 65–94.

[25] Steedman, Ian, 'The State and the outcome of the Pasinetti process', *The Economic Journal*, 1972, pp. 1387–95.

[26] Swan, T., 'Economic Growth and Capital Accumulation', *The Economic Record*, 1956, pp. 334–61.

[27] Vaughan, R. N., 'The Pasinetti Paradox in Neoclassical and More General Models: A Correction', *The Review of Economic Studies*, 1971, p. 271.

[28] Wood, Adrian, 'An Analysis of Income Distribution', University of Cambridge, 1972, unpublished Ph.D. thesis.

# Index

acceleration, principle of (or 'accelerator'), 48–51, 54, 56, 66; *see also* multiplier–accelerator

accumulation of capital: in Ricardo's theory, 6, 13–17; and capitalists' savings, 30, 112–13; and income distribution, 103, 113; capitalists' and workers' rate of, 122n, 129

Aftalion, Albert, 34, 48n

Alexander, Sidney S., 67

Allen, R. G. D., 60n, 83n

Anderson, James, 90

Balestra, Pietro, 144n

Baranzini, Mauro, 144n

Barkai, Haim, 17n

Baumol, William J., 60n

Bhaduri, Amit, 140n

Bickerdike, C. F., 48n

Böhm-Bawerk, Eugen von, 11, 144

Bonar, James, 87n, 88n

Bortkiewicz, Ladislaus von, 11n

Botero, Giovanni, 87n

Bruno, Michael, 146n

Bukharin, Nikolai, 34

Burmeister, Edwin, 146n

business fluctuations, *see* trade cycle

'Cambridge equation', 122, 127–8, 130, 131n, 134, 136–7, 139, 143

Cannan, Edwin, 89, 89n, 90n

capital intensity

uniformity of: crucial to Ricardo's theory of value, 3, 8, 20; also

capital intensity *continued*

crucial to determinateness of his system, 20–1

of U.S. economy, 92n

capital–output ratio, 48–9, 57–8, 64–5, 67, 75, 80, 93–7, 121, 124–7, 129–30; desired v. actual, 49, 57; determined independently of marginal productivities, 125; flexibility of, 114–5n, 122–5, 132–9; its constancy not essential to 'Cambridge equation', 128–30; and rate of profit, 123, 132–9

capital ownership, 106–7, 110, 127–8; share of, by workers and by capitalists, 108, 130, 141, 142

'capital stock adjustment' principle, 49, 57; *see also* acceleration, principle of

capitalist development: Ricardo's gloomy view of, 6, 15–17; Kaldor's more optimistic view of, 100–2

Carlyle, Thomas, 90n

causal ordering, 44–5, 115n; v. simultaneous equations, 44–8

Chenery, Hollis B., 57n

choice of technique, irrelevant to 'Cambridge equation', 115n, 126, 129–30

Clark, John Maurice, 48n

Clower, Robert F., 46n

Cobb–Douglas production function, 124n, 126n

Condorcet, Marquis de, 88

corn question, 89

Corry, B. A., 30n

investment: Keynes' theory of, 36–7; accelerator theory of, 48–50, 56; influencing effective demand and productive capacity in different ways, 93; equilibrium growth of, 68, 94–5; determining savings, 44–5, 52–3, 99n; sensitive to entrepreneurial expectations, 71; as an independent variable in the long run, 101, 103

Kahn, Richard F., Lord Kahn, 40, 104n, 145n
Kaldor, Nicholas, Lord Kaldor, 10n, 55n, 66, 69n, 97–102, 104–6, 113, 116, 118, 121, 122n, 143n; his theory of income distribution, 97–101, 104–6; his views on capitalist development, 95–7, 100–1; a 'logical slip', 106, 122n; on taxation, 97; and Ricardo, 101–2
Kalecki, Michal, 35, 55n, 66, 99n; on investment determining profits (and not the other way round), 99n
Keynes, John Maynard, Lord Keynes, 29–53, 54, 86, 87n, 92–5, 98, 99n, 100n, 102, 103, 134n; his 'general theory' of employment and income determination, 36–40; his methodology, 42–5; on Malthus, 31; and Classical economists, 42–5; and Ricardo, 42–4; distortions of, 45–8

Laing, Neil F., 140n
Lauderdale, James Maitland, Earl of, 34
Leijonhufvud, Axel, 46n
Leontief, Wassily W., 41–2
Levhari, David, 146n
liquidity-preference theory, 37–8; not essential to theory of effective demand, 47
Lloyd-George, David, 35
Lundberg, Erik, 50n
Luxembourg, Rosa, 34

macro-economic v. disaggregated analysis, 72–5, 118
McCulloch, John Ramsey, 3, 3n

Malthus, Thomas Robert, 3, 4n, 21, 29–31, 34, 34n, 43, 86–91, 92, 101, 102; on effective demand, 29–31; on population, 86–9; and Ricardo, 29–31
Manara, Carlo Felice, 79n
Mandeville, Bernard, 34n
Maneschi, Andrea, 122n
marginal efficiency of capital, 37; and Ricardian theory of rent, 43; v. marginal productivity, 43, 46
marginal productivity theory, 43, 122–6, 127–31, 132–3, 135n; and Keynes' marginal efficiency of capital, 43, 46
'market gluts', 29
Marrama, Vittorio, 55n, 66
Marris, Robin L., 143n
Marshall, Alfred, 17–18n, 35, 46n
Marx, Karl, 11n, 34, 35, 102, 144; on over-production, 34; on effective demand, 34n
Matthews, R. C. O., 49n
Meade, James E., 114n, 123n, 125n, 131n, 145n
Modigliani, Franco, 47n, 122n, 125n, 131n, 132n, 134, 135–6n, 137, 138, 142n, 143, 143n; *see also* Samuelson–Modigliani
Morishima, Michio, 135–6n, 137n, 145n
multiplier: 'instantaneous', 40, 45; 'lagged', 45, 51–3, 56
multiplier–accelerator interaction, 50, 54–75; limitations of, 50–1, 69–72
multi-sector models, 18–21, 41, 72–5, 118

'natural' prices v. market prices, 2, 4, 5
necessary (or wage-) goods v. luxury goods, 6, 11, 18–20; and basic v. non-basic commodities, 11n
Neisser, Hans, 70n

Ortes, Giammaria, 87n
over-production theories, 33–4

'paradoxes' (or results contrary to marginal productivity theory), 129–130, 129n, 146n